The *Magic* of Making Money on *eBay*®

GLOBAL
PUBLISHING
G R O U P

Global Publishing Group
Australia • New Zealand • Singapore • America • London

The
Magic
of Making Money on eBay ®

How we went from **broke** to **Millionaires** in under **2 years** & How **You** can too.

Matt & Amanda Clarkson

FIRST EDITION 2009

Copyright© 2010 Matt & Amanda Clarkson

National Library of Australia
Cataloguing-in-Publication entry:

Clarkson, Matt, 1971-
The Magic of Making Money On Ebay: How we went from broke to Millionaires in under 2 years & How You can too / Matt & Amanda Clarkson.

4th ed.
ISBN: 9781921630026 (pbk.)

1. eBay (Firm)
2. Internet auctions.
3. Internet marketing.
4. Electronic commerce.
5. Success in business.

Other Authors/Contributors:
Clarkson, Amanda, 1965-

381.177

Published by Global Publishing Group
PO Box 517 Mt Evelyn, Victoria, 3796, Australia
Email: info@TheGlobalPublishingGroup.com

For Further information about orders:
Phone: +61 3 9736 1156 or Fax: +61 3 8648 6871

GLOBAL
PUBLISHING
G R O U P

We dedicate this book to all the people who dare to believe that there is more out there for them in life and who have the courage, persistence and commitment to take action and to follow through on their journey until they achieve their dreams…

Matt & Amanda Clarkson

Acknowledgements

It has been an honour, a privilege, and a life goal achieved by writing this book. As with any major project or business success, there are many very special people who have contributed to our growth, making it possible for us to achieve our goals, and ultimately to making this book happen. So, we'd like to take this opportunity to say "THANK YOU".

Firstly, we'd like to thank our thousands of eBay Magic members who were the inspiration for this book.

Next, a huge thanks to our own wonderful in house dream team who support us while we work tirelessly to coordinate and pull all the material together for this book, as well as our ongoing efforts to spread the word on what's possible with an eBay business.

Thank you Genta Capan, Tamra Forde, Josh Clark, Grace Rados. You're an outstanding team and are the glue that holds this wild ride together!

We thank our friends and partners Darren & Jackie Stephens for their amazing talent, feedback and support.

A huge Thank You to our Awesome publisher Global Publishing Group for your dedication and commitment to the book's success.

I would also like to thank our loving family, friends and mentors Brett McFall, Mal Emery, Andrew & Daryl Grant, Mark Sneddon, Ravi Toor (Our eBay case manager), and Ken & Megsy for their constant support, laughter and encouragement… you're amazing.

Acknowledgements

And finally, we want to thank the people we admire and look up to, for their inspiration over our journey so far…Pierre Omidyar (eBay's founder), Donald Trump, Dr John DeMartini, Tony Robbins & Robert Kiyosaki. You have helped us grow and expanded our minds to the endless possibilities of business and life success.

Contents

Contents

THE **International**
Achievement INSTITUTE

Bringing Essential Knowledge & Book Summaries to High Achievers

I would like to personally congratulate you on investing in this valuable book. At The International Achievement Institute we continually strive to create excellence in the business world. And so it is with great pleasure that I write the foreword for this book. I believe it is a fantastic resource for anyone interested in making money or involved in business either as a start up or established business.

The online industry is one that is leading this country into greater economic prosperity and is central to the health of our economy. It is also an industry that is bringing incredible wealth and personal fulfilment to those involved in it. Critical to the success of our industry, its credibility, and its ability to weather the economic storms that may come, is not just good systems and methods, but most importantly good solid relationships.

Good relationships are, I believe, the difference between an outstanding business system and one that fails. I have seen this time and time again. And that is why this book is so valuable; because it is about people and their personal stories. Without the people behind them and their personal approach to relationships, a business owner is doomed to failure. With successful business-savvy people who know that 'relationship is king' involved in an eBay business, then the sky is the limit.

By learning from others and their mistakes you can be light years ahead of your competition. You can save hundreds of thousands of dollars simply by avoiding the mistakes they made and learned from.

The International Achievement Institute is proud to recommend this book as its authors are world leading eBay experts with many years of experience. They have taken on the ultimate challenge, made mistakes along the way, kept growing professionally and personally, and now enjoy incredible success.

As an International best selling author & consultant myself, I've had the privilege to consult and work with tens of thousands of people from Presidents, Rock stars, fortune 500 executives to every day people from all walks of life from over 27 countries.

For a few years I'd watched eBay growing as a company and I still didn't think of eBay as a serious business opportunity; I merely thought of it as a online junk yard. That was until I met Matt & Amanda Clarkson.

No business venture is without some level of risk, but by becoming more educated and informed you can reduce those risks so that they are far outweighed by the possible benefits.

This book will offer you just that information. It is an inspiring read and one that will make you want to jump out of your seat, leap out of your comfort zone and take action. And I encourage you to do just that.

Darren J. Stephens
Chief Executive Officer
The International Achievement Institute

Preface

What if you could start your own eBay business from scratch today (even if you have no idea what you're doing yet), have it up and running within hours, and even be making your first profits within 24 hours?

Sound too good to be true? Well, this is exactly what happened to us when we began our home-based eBay business back in February 2006 from the spare room of our apartment. We had absolutely no idea what we were doing (we'd never even been on the eBay website before) but what we did have was the burning desire in our stomach for a better life than we currently had.

We were prepared to do and learn anything to change our situation at the time and in fact we were running out of time fast. We were feeling stressed and uncertain about our financial future and knew that it was now or never...I was 40 years young and Matt was 34.

We'd had enough of the daily struggle (some would call it the rat race) and knew there was more to life than worrying about money and making sure we were going to be financially secure in our latter years. I'm sure you know what we mean.

And so we began our journey of finding a 'wealth vehicle' that would put an end to life on the rat wheel we despised...

Well, that was 3 years ago and today our life looks nothing like it did back then. Using eBay as our chosen 'wealth vehicle' we went on to build one of Australia's most successful eBay businesses, which now only takes around 10 hours a week to run. (Yes, we still have our eBay business to this day and will never give it up. ;-) Our eBay business

Preface

has given us not only the cash flow streams we craved, but time to do what we love the most, and that's now showing everyday people, just like you, exactly how we did it. Because, quite frankly, there's enough for all of us and our bigger purpose has gone far beyond just making money on eBay.

You're about to discover how two ordinary Aussies (a carpenter and a personal trainer) went from broke to eBay Millionaires in just 24 months and why we believe absolutely anyone, with any background whatsoever, who has a burning desire for a better, more enjoyable life, can do the same.

Let's begin the journey together…

REE BONUS

Claim Your
REE Report, Your
/D & Special
dio MP3 Gift
ith A Total Value
$297 visit...

w.biddingbuzz.com/book

"No matter where you are, no matter how difficult things might appear to be, you are always being moved toward magnificence. Always."

The Secret.

Chapter 1
Imagine If...

Chapter 1 : Imagine If...

We started our eBay business in February 2006, from absolute scratch, and within 8 months we were selling a minimum of $50,000 per month. The business now takes less than 10 hours a week to run because we've automated 90% of it. These days we still have our eBay business (we sell everyday physical items) but we spend most of our time on stage and traveling the world speaking about eBay, presenting seminars to help people like you become cash and time rich with eBay, and to demonstrate to them how they too can create multiple streams of income with eBay.

One important aspect of our eBay business is the fun we've had and continue to have, especially in the presentation of our seminars. You see, when you're having fun and loving every moment of what you do, the line between work and play becomes blurred and this, my friend, is the real secret to long lasting happiness and fulfillment.

> **The business now takes less than 10 hours a week to run because we've automated 90% of it.**

In this book you're about to discover how you can start an eBay business from scratch today and start profiting instantly - even if you've never sold a thing on eBay before. Basically this book is all about helping you discover a whole range of possibilities that are out there with eBay, as we take you through a proven and very successful process, that we've gone through ourselves, to get to where we are today with our eBay business.

To claim your **FREE** report and DVD (valued $97) go to
www.biddingbuzz.com/book

You'll see how you could exponentially increase your income, quickly and easily, using advanced tips, proven strategies and jealously guarded secrets that could turn you into the next eBay millionaire.

Did you know that currently around 1.3 million people now earn their primary or secondary living selling all sorts of things to people, all over the world, on eBay?

Not only that, more than 78 million eBay members spend a staggering $141 million every single day on eBay! This equates to US $1 billion being spent on eBay every week of the year. (Could you see yourself with even a small slice of that pie?)

> ## "More than 78 million eBay members spend a staggering $141 million every single day on eBay!"

Just to give you an idea of how massive and untapped the eBay opportunity is, take a close look at the following statistics and begin to imagine what it would be like if you were one of the sellers who enjoy incredible incomes thanks to this phenomenal platform, eBay.

- There are approximately 6.4 million items added every day

- Over 30,000 fashion items are sold every day

- There are 78 million items available worldwide

- Over 2,000 bids are placed on antiques & artwork every hour

- Every 20 seconds, a piece of women's clothing sells.

- Nearly 78 million eBay users spend $141 million every day!

- Most eBay sellers are everyday people who sell everything imaginable

- At any given moment, eBay is conducting some 12 million auctions, divided into about 18,000 categories

- The most expensive item sold on eBay to date is a private business jet for US$4.9 million

- Over 7,600 gold pieces are sold every week

- A craft item is sold every 9 seconds

- 95% of sellers on eBay are individuals or small businesses

- A laptop is sold every 13 minutes

- A stamp is sold every 2 minutes, 54 seconds

- An antique is sold every 5 minutes, 8 seconds

- A baby item is sold every 5 minutes

- An item of sports memorabilia is sold every 1 minute, 21 seconds

- A computer game is sold every 1 minute, 16 seconds

- A DVD is sold every 34 seconds

- A toy is sold every 24 seconds

- A piece of women's clothing is sold every 20 seconds

To claim your **FREE** report and DVD (valued $97) go to
www.biddingbuzz.com/book

Thousands of eBay sellers around the world are quietly making a small fortune selling things on eBay - yet you'd never know.

In fact, there are now over 178,000 people in the UK now using eBay for their primary or secondary source of income.

They simply keep their secret close to their chests and continue to bank large sums of money every day of the week.

Most eBay sellers are everyday people who sell everything imaginable - notice that last point? They are everyday people just like you.

And maybe just like you, they too were once caught up in the rat race of life and looking for a better, smarter and fun way to make money from the comfort of their own homes, or even just adding extra streams of income to help make things easier. Maybe enjoy a few more choices instead of having to settle for less all the time.

The only difference between these people and you is they have already discovered the golden opportunity eBay has to offer and decided to jump off the treadmill of drudgery and do something about it.

Are you fed up with having to drag yourself out of bed each morning and head off to a job you hate with a passion, or don't really care about?

> **"Most eBay sellers are everyday people who sell everything imaginable"**

Or perhaps you already own a business that isn't all it's cracked up to be and now you're a slave to it, working more hours than ever before, driving yourself into the ground! Who knows – you're probably paying your staff more than you're paying yourself and doing twice as many hours?

When was the last time you actually woke up, and felt excited about starting the day ahead of you? We mean really excited?

If you had to stop for a moment and think about it, then it's definitely time to do something about it - and fast. In fact…it's an emergency!

How would your life be different than it is today if you had plenty of extra cash at the end of the week, to be able to enjoy the finer things in life, instead of just having enough to get you through till next pay day?

Who knows? Maybe you're already comfortable but so time-poor you never even get to enjoy it? What's the point of it all? The weeks all seem to blend, and with the hours most people are having to work, just so they can pay their bills, it's little wonder so many are looking for a better, smarter way to become cash and time rich.

Imagine yourself being able to enjoy so many more things in life that are out of your immediate reach right now. How would you feel if you didn't have to live on a tight weekly budget and could be spontaneous occasionally, and experience things in life, as they happen to pop up? All without having to worry whether or not you can afford it. How would that be?

Imagine if you could stop working full time in your current job and have your own highly profitable eBay business running from your spare bedroom or kitchen table.

To claim your **FREE** report and DVD (valued $97) go to
www.biddingbuzz.com/book

Or even if you didn't want to stop what you're doing right now, how about some extra income streams of cash flow coming into your bank account each day. Would this make a difference to you and your family today?

Even if you just replaced your current income, would you rather be hanging at home, making money, having fun or doing what you're already doing? We bet we know the answer to that!

And, if you do currently have your own business, how about being able to sell old or surplus stock on eBay and creating another lucrative stream of income? There are thousands of eBay sellers who do this, and actually make more money on eBay than they do in their bricks and mortar business! (We know this as we have customers who are doing this day in, day out).

Would these extra streams of easy income make quite a difference to your current situation? What about being able to have a long weekend every week?

You could spend the extra time doing things you actually enjoy, like gardening, shopping, relaxing, going to the beach, spending more time with each other and the kids, visiting friends, wining and dining with your better half, exercising, going to the movies during the day, whatever. All the things you have to put on the backburner because you don't have the time or the money today.

Meanwhile life could be passing you by, one day at a time.

Whatever you're doing right now, stop and take a moment out for yourself and imagine this…

Next Monday morning, instead of getting up early and battling the traffic, you wake up at a time that suits you.

Since starting your eBay business, you never experience 'Mondayitis' ever again!

You fly out of bed every morning feeling charged up and ready to enjoy your day. You're smiling just thinking about the money that will have appeared in your bank account while you've been asleep.

You have a leisurely breakfast, boot up your computer, and then you go right to your eBay account and see how much money you've made over night or the past 24 hours.

Time seems to stand still. Your blood starts pumping as you realize you've made more money in the past 24 hours than you used to make all bloody week, *slaving* away and getting no thanks for it!

And best of all…you hardly had to a lift a finger, because your eBay business is now mostly automated. You're now working part-time and making more money than you ever have before. Life is good and you feel in total control of your financial destiny. Finally.

In truth, you almost feel guilty because it was too easy and you've never had it *this* easy before! Your efforts are now paying off. Big time.

You feel a wave of gratitude and certainty wash over you because you now have the 'secret step by step recipe' to making unstoppable cash flow streams on eBay and your only boundaries and limits to the amount of money you make are those in your own mind…

To claim your **FREE** report and DVD (valued $97) go to
www.biddingbuzz.com/book

Your biggest job for the day is to decide whether to grow and expand your eBay business, to bring in even more money, or to simply enjoy the lifestyle you've longed for, for so damn long.

You now sleep soundly every single night and never ever wake up with knots in your stomach wondering how the hell you'll be able to pay all the mounting bills. In fact, you never have to worry about money again.

You know how to make as much as you want because you have the proven system in your hands just as if you had next Saturday nights lotto numbers, but even better, because you can do it over and over again if you choose to…

How does this make you feel?
Well then let's explore how this is all done…

Matt and Amanda
Bidding Buzz Ltd

"We've got but one shot at life, let's take it while we're still not afraid. Because life is so brief, and time is a thief, when you're undecided. And like a fistful of sand, it can slip right through your hands…"

Rod Stewart, 'Young Turks'

Chapter 2
All The Gear and No Idea

Chapter 2 : All The Gear And No Idea

When we first met, we were virtually dead broke. Absolutely broke. I had less than nothing because I had over $5000 in credit card debt. Amanda also had nothing and was driving around in her tired, rusty, 1980-something mobile pie van, which was called the 'Pie Princess'. The 'Pie Princess' (as her customers fondly called her in the early days) delivered home cooked food and goodies to factory workers and construction sites, all around our city, twice a day.

Let's just say that the actual food van wasn't that flash (it was well and truly on it's last legs) but it was always spotlessly clean and the food was always fresh and delicious. In fact, the poor old van was so broken down, that one day Amanda went to open the door and it literally fell off while she was trying to serve food to all the hungry guys on a busy building site. Embarrassing to say the least, but of course she had plenty of offers to fix it on the spot, and off she went to the next stop. She was always racing against the clock (the workers also being on strict break times) so there was never time for stuffing around, as she'd politely put it! There was money to be made and little time to do it, as the competition in her area was getting tough.

The food business was a hard slog, with long working hours, and lots of hard work 6 days a week. After 3 years of getting up at 4am, cooking till 7.30am, then driving to 22 different scheduled food stops 5 days a week, Amanda had hit the wall and basically just couldn't face another day of cooking rissoles, pies, casseroles, and the other 30 different dishes she had on offer anymore.

By the time 3 years had passed, she was so stuffed and angry at where she was at in life, that her regulars had started calling her the 'Pie Witch' instead of the 'Pie Princess'. She knew she had to get out…and fast. Things were looking bleak. She was dog tired, feeling older, still almost broke and felt clueless at the ripe old age of 31.

Meanwhile, I spent many years on the tools, wondering exactly what it was I really wanted to do with my life. I finished my apprenticeship as a carpenter at 19 and was a registered builder by the age of 21, and yet I just knew that I really didn't want to keep working in that trade. I wanted to do more, but I had a lot of family and friends saying, "You've put so much into it. You're a builder now. Don't let it go. Don't waste what you've already achieved."

So I stuck with it for another eleven years after my apprenticeship finished, even though I didn't enjoy what I was doing. The truth was, I hated it. I was listening to other well-meaning friends and family who really weren't giving the right advice for me.

So, when Amanda and I got together, we had no clue about making money. Amanda is six years older than me, but at that stage she was no closer to understanding how to make money and create assets for the long term than I was.

But, ultimately it was fine, because for us, we began the process together with nothing. We were starting our journey at our 'financial ground zero' but were so ready for the changes we knew were ahead for us.

After about a year or so into the relationship, and still trying to figure it all out, we read Robert Kiyosaki's book, Rich Dad, Poor Dad.

When we first read that book, it was like, "Where has this whole understanding of the financial world been all our lives?"

We didn't have any clue about making money; our parents hadn't taught us anything about making money, so we had to discover it for ourselves. We felt as though we had discovered gold at the time and secretly felt excited beyond belief that ordinary people like us could actually create wealth, simply by following someone else's step-by-step success steps. Finally we had a feeling our lives were going to take a dramatic change for the better.

> **"Ordinary people like us could actually create wealth, simply by following someone else's step-by-step success steps."**

As we read this book our minds were being opened to ideas for making money we never thought possible or knew existed. We thought, "Gee, maybe one day we could start a company or something?"

I was 25 at this stage and I had no idea what I was doing. I was building houses every day for wealthy people and I still didn't know that I should own one. It just hadn't occurred to me if you can believe that!

That very afternoon (after we'd finished the book in one day) we set out on a journey and decided we should go and buy a house. I had no money, as I said, and a $5000 credit card debt. So I spent the next 10 months working 12-hour days, six days a week getting our first home deposit together.

I also had to drive an hour and a half each way to get to the larger construction sites I was working on at the time. It was hard, but we were on a mission, and nothing was going to stop us.

I'd get up in the morning and had to be on site, swinging a hammer, at 6:30am, an hour-and-a-half drive from where I was living. To do this I had to set my alarm for 4:15am, but because it was so early and

I used to have trouble getting up that early day after day, I would set the time forward on the clock so it was showing two hours ahead. I was actually tricking my brain when I woke up so that I was seeing 6:15am when in reality it was only 4:15am.

I played little tricks on my brain like that, because I really wasn't enjoying what I was doing. I'd then drive to work with my rechargeable razor in one hand and a coffee in the other. I was hating every minute on the building sites, swinging a hammer, knocking my already bad back around and making it even worse. I turned my mind to buying our first home and it really did get me through those long months.

I need to clarify here that I had many good friends on the construction sites and the great people and characters I worked with helped make it bearable. At times we had a lot of fun and many laughs along the way, so it wasn't all bad.

At the end of those 10 months of working 6 days a week we had paid off our debts and saved up a $14,000 deposit. We realized back then that $14,000 wasn't going to get us our dream home but we had to start somewhere. This was also long before the sub prime mortgage disaster hit, where you still needed a decent deposit and a savings history to get a home loan.

We decided on a budget of $110,000; we could afford the repayments and not place ourselves in a position of too much stress. I let Amanda know how much we could spend and off she went in search of our first 'dream home'. Although she set out to stick to the budget, she actually found a place we both really wanted where they were asking $135,000. Typical!

Now, if you're familiar with coastal towns, people try to get as close to the beach as they can (it's always been our dream to live as close to the beach as possible). If you can get on the eastern side of the highway living on the east coast of Australia, then you're on the 'beach-side' and that's where most people really want to be.

The little beachside apartment was in a 30-year old apartment building containing just 6 units. It was everything we wanted at that time, but even then it was going to be a massive stretch for us and we both knew it.

I told Amanda, "I don't know if we can afford this." And she replied, "I reckon we can stretch it. Let's do it. Let's put an offer in."

Somehow she talked me into it as she always does. With her positive 'can do' attitude towards life, she wasn't going to take no for an answer this time!

So, we put the offer in and ended up buying this place at $131,000. Yes, above budget by $21,000, but we would make it work somehow.

We had just bought our very first home together and the feeling was one of real achievement and a step in the right direction for a change.

Unfortunately, not long after we moved into this place, there was a bit of a downturn in the building industry on the Gold Coast and for a while I wasn't getting any work. Of course, panic and concern soon set in. As a 'hands on' carpenter if I'm not on the tools swinging a hammer then I'm not making any money. I worked for myself so I had no employee benefits. No holiday pay, no sick pay, no superannuation. Nothing.

So, for me, it was like, right, I need to do something about this. Here we were, we'd bought this place, and all of a sudden I found myself out of work. Great.

To claim your **FREE** report and DVD (valued $97) go to
www.biddingbuzz.com/book

By now we were in our first home and we were literally sitting at the kitchen table, I can still remember it clearly, counting out five and ten cent pieces from a plastic container for a loaf of bread.

It was a pretty sad and pathetic state to be in. We had no money, we weren't working (Amanda had consequently got out of the pie van business) and we started to really doubt ourselves and wonder just what we had done.

Amanda was 32 by now and I was desperate. It was embarrassing for both of us and we hated every minute of it. We discussed it at length and thought if we don't do something different, we'll wake up in 10 or 20 years and nothing will have changed.

> ## "We've had the doubting Thomas' laugh at us when we dared to share our dreams"

Amanda had really thought that by then, she would at least be well on the way to having all that she'd ever wanted. Not that she'd ever put any thought into exactly how it was going to happen. No one who knows us could say we don't know what it's like to struggle, because we do. We've been there. We've had the heartaches and sleepless nights. We've had the doubting Thomas' laugh at us when we dared to share our dreams but we also knew we didn't want to be 'broke and desperate' ever again.

Despite the setbacks we kept a positive mind, took action and we pushed forward. I finally got back into working, when it was there, and started making a little bit of money.

> ## "Despite the setbacks we kept a positive mind, took action and we pushed forward"

To progress our lives even further, I found myself asking, "What are my skills?" My skills at that stage were building and renovating, so we started to renovate our own property. We renovated that one and after 18 months of working night times and weekends, we sold it and made about $23,000 profit on it.

At that time it was a massive improvement - we couldn't believe that we had made this amount of money in only 18 months. We truly thought we were pretty hot and on the road to riches.

It turned out this was also the beginning of the renovation boom in Australia; everybody was renovating, all the renovation shows were on TV and it was all gung ho.

We went on to do seven successful and profitable renovations in a row. At the time, everyone was doing houses so we targeted beachfront apartments up and down the Gold Coast. What was good for us was I had the skills to be able to do everything myself. Everything from the tiling, concreting, plastering to painting, you name it I did it.

Amanda had the complimentary and very helpful skills of telling me what to do, while looking over my shoulder, and letting me know in her expert opinion if something was too rough or if it passed muster - clearly she knew best.

Her family is in the building trade also, so everything was compared to how it would have been done if her father and brothers had done it. Can you imagine what I had to go through? I still laugh at it now.

We got to the stage where we were successfully renovating property and could have kept going, but we faced the problem of still not having a lot of cash.

It felt like we were forever without any money in our pockets, spending money just to buy new building materials or tools. Frustrating.

One gorgeous day, it was New Years Day 2003, I was looking down over the beach, in front of our apartment, watching everyone on holiday and having fun in the sun. We lived right on a great surfing beach in Burleigh Heads on the Gold Coast, which was absolutely packed with holiday makers and locals lapping up the sun and just loving life.

I'm thinking…all this fun outside while I was sanding plasterboard above my head in the lounge room, which looked directly over this scene on the beach.

It was so hot (about 35 degrees Celsius and very humid) and I was literally covered in perspiration and the plaster dust was falling all over me. I was sanding away and becoming more pissed off by the minute; because of the heat and my discomfort from perspiration, the plaster dust was actually drying and resetting on my body, which meant that as I was sanding the plaster, it was cracking and every time I moved I was making a crackle, crackle, crackle sound. All the while I was looking down at everyone having fun on the beach.

I felt sick with envy and resented where we were at in our lives even more, because we still felt as though we had no spare money even though we were now at it 7 days a week.

Worse still, while we were renovating this particular property, we had to set up the toaster on top of the toilet cistern (very sexy) because every other part of the unit was gutted and it was the only room left with a power point. On top of that, one day over the busy Christmas holiday period, I accidentally jack hammered too far into the concrete floor and severed the intercom lines for the whole building.

Picture this; we were on the 11th floor of the high-rise and were told by a very agitated manager that the noise and vibration could be heard and felt all the way down into the basement. She was getting complaint after complaint she angrily informed us. What, did she think; we were actually enjoying ourselves up there and laughing along while we worked? (I really mean, while I worked with Amanda's help).

Unfortunately the lines I severed shut the whole intercom system down in the building for days and it being the Christmas / New Year break it sent the whole building into a turmoil. At one stage, the manager burst into tears and said it was our fault that people were checking out early and that they stood to lose a lot of money.

Of course, they never thanked us when we increased the value of the other units in the block by at least $90,000 when we sold the unit at a record price that everyone said we'd never get! For many years this was our seven-day a week routine. When I wasn't on the tools working, I'd come home and I would work until 9 or 10 o'clock at night renovating and trying to create a better life.

We got to the point where, even though we felt like we were getting ahead, we really weren't, because we had no spare liquid cash, so we really wanted to figure out how we could make more money and have more cash flow. That's really where we started the process of moving outside what we were currently doing. We started investigating and doing different, smaller businesses.

To claim your **FREE** report and DVD (valued $97) go to
www.biddingbuzz.com/book

Also, from my previous experience seeing a building boom and bust in the housing industry in 1991 - 1992, I knew right away when the reserve bank lifted interest rates, two months in a row, that the market was going to change.

I said to Amanda that we had to sell our final project that we were living in before the market changed and everyone was trying to get out at the same time.

So we sold that beachfront unit for a building record of $600, 000 when other units were still selling for around $450,000 and waited to see what would happen to the market. Sure enough a downturn came and many people were left with high debts to service as many of them felt that the market was just going to keep going up.

Due to the market changing we were actually back at square 1, again, when it came to looking at finding a way to create more equity and cash flow. Our only source of growth had stopped for now and we didn't know how to do anything else.

I'll let Amanda tell her part of the story now, as she needs to get her words out for the day…
Hi, I'm from Tasmania and one of five kids who grew up in a normal, hard working-class family. Although my parents never really taught us anything about business and making money, thankfully they did get us into athletics when we were very young. My dad Peter was a pro cyclist and a solid plasterer by trade, while my mum, Pam, was a great homemaker, who looked after foster children, and also a fantastic runner in her early years.

Growing up I was always looking for ways to make money. I was prepared to do all sorts of chores, anything really, as long as I got money! I would even climb into Mum's washing machine, after she had washed Dad's overalls each night, looking for loose change that had fallen from his pockets.

Here's me at 11 prospecting for gold in the washing machine.

Now that's Venture Capital Tassie style!

Then I'd spend the bootie on mixed lollies, back in the days when they were still four lollies for a cent! Remember those days? I'd come home with bags and bags and cut the lollies up into little pieces, bag them up and then sell them back to my family at night while they were watching TV. I even made myself one of those cardboard trays to display the treats on and hung it around my neck. I really thought I had a serious business going on.

They used to laugh at me even back then, but I would invest every cent back into buying more and more stock. That bit I worked out

To claim your **FREE** report and DVD (valued $97) go to
www.biddingbuzz.com/book

myself! I would even tap dance for my aunty Patsy for less than ten cents an hour. Apparently I don't have any rhythm, according to Mum, so they laughed at my efforts for hours on end. Nice. This went on for years and Mum said I was always a goer and would one day have a 'real' business.

I left school at 16 after having failed every subject except religion and art. Go figure! On top of that, I was constantly told I was dumb and would never amount to much. Not by my parents, but from those who I looked up to and believed in. I carried these beliefs for years, and they affected many of my early decisions, until I decided I wasn't going to let them ruin my life.

Thankfully, certain people came into my life who helped me change my whole mindset. More on that later though.

When I was 24, my whole family moved to the Gold Coast to get away from the freezing Tasmanian weather.

We're a close-knit family so it worked out for all of us. I quickly got into competing in triathlons and just loved the whole healthy lifestyle the Gold Coast had to offer. It was a fun, crazy life, training, competing, hanging out with my friends and I never really gave any thought to my future at all, to tell you the truth!

I wasn't really into working for anyone else and, by the time I'd reached 30 years of age, I'd actually had 33 different jobs. I just couldn't find my niche in life and always knew I had to keep moving on till I found my groove, so to speak. I didn't think twice about changing jobs because being happy and fulfilled was far higher on my values list. I knew I had to have my own business, so that's what I went for.

I started the Pie Van business when I was 30, single and carefree. Actually, the truth is, I started this business in the hope of meeting a good looking guy and making new friends. A bit silly, I know, but I didn't think anything of it. I thought I'd make a few sandwiches, meet some guys and have fun for the day. Yeah right! Well, you already know how that ended!

The most positive gift that came out of that business, after those three years, is that I did meet my husband to be, Matt, so it was well worth it. On top of that he was 6 years younger, so I was very pleased with myself ;-)

After the Pie Princess days were over, along with the renovating days, we became involved in a video rental business and after that I studied and became a Personal Trainer.

Being a Personal Trainer actually met a lot of my needs, both physically and mentally, and I grew a very successful business over the course of the next few years. I seemed to have a knack for empowering people to be their best and thoroughly enjoyed helping and guiding them along the way with my firm methods.

"At the end of the day, I was still trading time for dollars"

However, at the end of the day, I was still trading time for dollars, but more importantly, I knew I had not yet reached my full potential. What that potential was at the time I had no idea. I just felt it. Matt and I would talk about this often but never in a million years was I prepared for what happened next!

He came home one day and announced he had discovered the right business for us, one that would meet all our needs and give us the life we had been dreaming of for years. It was going to be an Internet Business!

Now, I'm a hands-on person. I left school when I was sixteen, in 1982, so my computer skills were stretched just using a calculator. Here I was at 37 and had never even sent an email, let alone owned a computer - and Matt comes home and says we're going to start an Internet business.

"What the (expletive deleted) are you talking about?" I asked in shock.

Luckily I'm a positive, open-minded person, so the least I could do was to pour myself a big glass of wine and listen to what Matt had to say about this Internet stuff. I was that desperate for the 'answers'.

Matt believes he has the answers so I'll let him tell this part...

I spent many years working on luxury homes in exclusive up market estates so I was constantly around wealthy people and seeing how they lived. One day I was working on a jobsite at an exclusive water front estate, a massive multi-million dollar mansion, on the Gold Coast.

That was the day I had what I call my 'defining' moment, when I knew everything had to change, because what I was doing wasn't taking me closer to my goals and dreams of wealth and success. I want to describe it to you in detail so you can get a perspective of how I felt at that time.

I was eating lunch and sitting on my customary seat I had made out of the concrete building blocks used to build the house. We would make a lunch spot out of whatever we had at hand, usually a few bricks piled on top of each other, or off cuts of timber laid across more sticks or bricks. We'd try to get out of the sun, but often there was no roof on as yet, so we were constantly in the elements getting sun burnt or wind blown.

I'd cover myself in sunscreen, although I was constantly getting sun spots burnt off, and because I was always cutting and drilling timber I'd always be covered in sawdust.

This would then get stuck in the sunscreen, which created a sticky thick layer of gunk on your arms, neck and face. I'd think to myself… "How the hell did I end up here?" With every passing day, on those building sites, I grew more and more resentful with my lot in life. I was cutting wood all day, but daydreaming of a better life, and knew I couldn't stomach this for much longer.

This particular day, while sitting there, eating my dusty jam and cheese sandwiches, this massive boat came into sight and stopped at the water pontoon, in front of the house we were working on.

Now, I didn't know much about super yachts, but this boat was longer than the land we were building the house on. The boat owner was the person we were building the mansion for and he and his family were living on the boat for the entire year we'd take to build his house.

I was constantly around these wealthy people, observing them closely, and I always had an abiding curiosity about what they did and how they made their money.

Not really knowing anything about creating wealth, I always thought to myself, "Somehow these people are making vast amounts of money and if they can do it, then surely I can too?"

I just didn't know how – not yet!

Enough was enough so I asked this wealthy guy how he'd made his money. Usually in that type of situation I'd just chat with the owners and be as helpful as I could, bearing in mind I was just the carpenter doing the timberwork, I wasn't the head contractor or builder.

So I struck up a conversation with the owner and learnt he was originally from Canada but had moved out to Australia to retire. I gathered he was still only in his 40's. I found the nerve to ask him how he had made his fortune and he told me that he had made it by creating software that was used and sold over the Internet.

Now, I had no clue what he was talking about at the time as I had barely even used a computer.

"Wow, the Internet,"I thought,"this is something new, something out there, with so much buzz in the news about the Internet, surely there has got to be something there for me too?"

I need to clarify at this point that being a tradesman is a great way to create a living and I know many successful people who can provide for themselves and their families working on the tools. There is nothing wrong with working with your hands, I just knew that it ultimately wasn't for me and that there had to be an easier, more profitable way, for me to get ahead. There were only so many hours in the day, which meant there were only so many hours I could charge for working hands on.

I had a dream at the time of making $2000 a week in passive income. That was my goal. I didn't know how. I didn't know what I'd do with the money. I just knew that I wanted to wake up and have money coming in even if I chose not to work that day. That was my goal.

After talking with the man with the huge boat, and massive house under construction, I decided maybe the Internet was the place to look. That's when I went home to Amanda and said, "I've got to do something different. I don't know what, or how yet, but things have to change."

At that stage I was what some people call a 'gunna' - I'm 'gunna' do this, I'm 'gunna' to do that. But up until then I hadn't done anything to change my life. Thankfully Amanda was reasonably patient with my 'gunna' attitude and supportive in her own way.

When I came home that day, I told Amanda what I wanted to do about making money on the internet and she cracked it and said "You're always 'gunna' do this and 'gunna' do that. For God's sake, just do something or stop your bloody whinging! I'm sick of you going on with all your ideas and doing nothing about it!"

To claim your **FREE** report and DVD (valued $97) go to
www.biddingbuzz.com/book

Exactly how I expected her to respond. No surprises there.

Anyway I told her that I was going to stop being this 'gunna' person. "I'm going to stop being this person who had all these ideas, had all these dreams, and has not followed through with them."

I realized that I needed to do something serious. I needed to make a change in myself so that I could truly reach the potential I saw for my life. And that's when I made the serious decision to sell all of my tools. As a carpenter I needed them to work with every day to make my living. I thought to myself, "I can't come back to these tools; if I don't do something drastic, I'm going to be here in another 20 years time."

> **"I'm going to stop being this person who had all these ideas, had all these dreams, and has not followed through with them."**

We had a mortgage to pay, bills mounting up every week, like everyone else does, and I had a wife who loved to buy shoes. Luckily, Amanda was as keen as I was for a better life, so she trusted my gut feeling and went along with what I did next.

I sold all my tools plus another investment property we had a bit of equity in, to fund this new adventure. We were that serious.

"You're going to pay for your education one way or another… Time or Money. You just need to decide… which is less painful for you."

Mal Emery…mentor and friend

To claim your **FREE** report and DVD (valued $97) go to
www.biddingbuzz.com/book

Chapter 3
If It's To Be, It's Up To Me

Chapter 3 : If It's To Be, It's Up To Me

Because we were coming from such a low base of knowledge (zero actually), we knew that we had to begin the journey of educating ourselves. At the time I also had a friend who was quickly becoming an Internet expert on how to use the Internet to make money. It really is amazing how things start 'to happen' once you 'put it out there' as they say.

I called this friend and asked him what should I do if I wanted to get into the Internet? He told me I needed to begin educating myself on how to do it and also told me about a number of seminars I should attend in the United States, as they are well ahead of us here in Australia. So we flew to Nashville, in America, and went to an Internet marketing seminar that had a whole line up of speakers with different skills and experiences. Each of the seminar speakers would have an hour and a half, to explain the concept of their success on the Internet, and at the end of their time on stage they would give you the opportunity to purchase their individual system.

All this was so amazing and new to us. We just had no clue people would be able to find such a vast array of professionals in a field, who could show you how to learn from them, and replicate what they have been able to do. That was the beginning of our journey of educating ourselves so we could fast track our results and learn from people who had already blazed the trail before us.

We had a lot of mixed results when we first started selling on the Internet and we certainly weren't breaking any records. We were just sort of figuring it out as we went along. And luckily I had a supportive partner who was there with me all along the journey.

To claim your **FREE** report and DVD (valued $97) go to
www.biddingbuzz.com/book

> **"So, you have to ask yourself - and you might want to write your answer down - what are you prepared to do to do, to change your current situation?"**

We were prepared to sell our only asset to educate ourselves. So, you have to ask yourself - and you might want to write your answer down - what are you prepared to do to do, to change your current situation? Because, if you don't do something different, nothing is going to happen and you'll wake up in years to come, possibly no better off than you are now.

We were running out of time fast, and spending money was far less painful than time wasted, trying to work it out for

> **"We were running out of time fast"**

ourselves. We'd already lost enough of that.

We sold a block of five units to get the money to educate ourselves because we didn't learn this stuff at school. No one else is going to teach you or educate you. It's up to you to find your right mentors, and follow in their proven steps, because no one cares about your outcome like you should.

We have a saying, and you might want to write this down. "Never ask the opinion of someone who does not have the result you want, because they are just not qualified."

It's the biggest lesson we've ever received through the benefit of having mentors. It will mean gaining new friends and losing many old ones along the way, so be prepared. Your friends and family don't want you to change…it makes them feel uncomfortable, so they'll often try and talk you into sticking to 'what you know best.' What, best for them, or best for you?

When it comes to mentoring advice, your relatives and well-meaning friends are probably clueless unless they have outstanding success in the area you're interested in. If your parents, your brothers, sisters, your best friends, haven't got what you want, don't ask for their advice on what you want to do. In fact, don't even mention it, because if we'd listened to those who 'reckoned' they knew better and that making money on the Internet was a scam or impossible, we'd still be bloody broke!

Back to finding the answer…

> **"Never ask the opinion of someone who does not have the result you want, because they are just not qualified."**

As I was saying, we were having mixed results making money, the new, traditional way as Internet marketers. That's where you build a website, drive traffic (potential customers) to it, begin the process of marketing to gain their confidence and finally sell something to them, either a physical product or information.

While I understood and enjoyed this process, Amanda really struggled with the whole concept and just didn't enjoy it.

To claim your **FREE** report and DVD (valued $97) go to
www.biddingbuzz.com/book

Mainly because, as a woman, she needed certainty when it came to knowing how much money was coming into our account on a weekly basis.

She liked to plan and know that a certain amount was coming in, week in and week out. With Internet marketing it's kind of hard to know how much money you'll make, because it depends on the sales you make through your own marketing abilities.

No matter how hard she tried, she just didn't get it, nor did she like it. She was once again feeling frustrated and worried about time ticking by, but I wasn't about to give up. Not by a long shot.

And then the answer finally appeared from out of the blue…

"The greatest revolution in our generation is the discovery that human beings, by changing the inner attitudes of their minds, can change the outer aspects of their lives"

William James

Chapter 4
Accidental Gold Mine

Chapter 4 : Accidental Gold Mine

Quite by accident, one day in February 2006, we discovered eBay and it was the turning point in our life. The lights in Amanda's head went on instantly when she was on the eBay website and could see, from the information available, that anyone who put their heart and mind into this business could, quite literally, make a fortune.

It was simple to understand, very little risk, the customers where there, and best of all, they were spending a massive one billion dollars plus a week!

You see, with eBay, you don't have to get your own traffic (customers) to the website like you do with traditional Internet marketing. This is all taken care of, and all you need to do is sell things that people want. It's simple really…the whole eBay website is run on the 'supply vs demand' philosophy. In other words, sell things people want to buy and you're in business!

> **"You see, with eBay, you don't have to get your own traffic (customers) to the website like you do with traditional Internet marketing"**

This made perfect sense to both of us (Amanda was on a high because she'd finally found the missing link) and we wasted no time in getting the best mentors in the world to fast track the process and get us into the top 5% of sellers who really know how to make the money. And fast.

During those first few months of being mentored and learning the ropes, we were making around $800 a week net profit, selling

To claim your **FREE** report and DVD (valued $97) go to
www.biddingbuzz.com/book

everything around the house that wasn't nailed down. Mainly books, DVD's, CD's and video's as well as house hold bits and pieces.

> **"During those first few months of being mentored and learning the ropes, we were making around $800 a week net profit, selling everything around the house that wasn't nailed down"**

I think the turning point for us was the fact that we were making money within 48 hours of putting up our first auction on eBay and although we made many mistakes we still made a profit of $133.50. Not much I know, but for Amanda it was proof that absolutely anyone could do this; we got instant financial gratification which in turn gave us even more hope and determination and, with the right mentoring, we knew we could quickly and easily get out of the rat race we were in.

> **"We were making money within 48 hours of putting up our first auction on eBay"**

There was no stopping us. We were at it daily and the money just kept rolling in. We were having a ball and we'd never been as happy. Amanda got to know everyone at the post office, which was all she really had to do each day. (Could you handle that? ;-) We even took a trip to America and we brought along some books and DVD's we were selling on eBay, so we didn't have to shut the business down. We were selling in America anyway, so we simply posted them out as we sold them. In fact, most of our sales happened while we were sitting on the plane, high in the sky! Gotta love that!

We got serious, found new, untapped markets, and worked diligently on building and growing it into a very lucrative business. Within 8 months, from a standing start, we were making more money than we ever had before.

We'd automated our daily tasks to the point where it was now taking less than 10 hours a week to run. The automation process was incredible to us, because never before had we had so much spare time on our hands.

We were no longer selling books and things, but had found our 'niche' market after doing our research, and to this day, we still sell the same physical things after three years. The beauty of our business is that we've created a saleable asset, because it no longer requires us to do any daily tasks.

To claim your **FREE** report and DVD (valued $97) go to
www.biddingbuzz.com/book

Chapter 5
When Your Dreams Become Your Reality…

Chapter 5 : When Your Dreams…

"Be careful what you wish for…
The universe works in
Magical & Mysterious ways."

Matt & Amanda Clarkson

"All I (Matt) want is an easy business that
makes me around $2,500 profit every week
on the Internet, doing a few hours work, but
mostly all automated. Just something boring and
uncomplicated where I don't have to think too
much, but something that's fun too."

This was in December 2005.

It was now August 2006…

Here's how our days would pan out. We'd get up around 6am (Amanda was still the task master) and we'd train for an hour each morning. We lived in a lovely apartment overlooking the blue Pacific Ocean on the Gold Coast.

It was Amanda's dream view. She lived for her running. She'd run barefoot on the soft sand for about 10km, go for an ocean swim and lift weights. I'd go to the gym and do my thing. I loved my 'cave time' each morning and I always looked forward to getting home afterwards, to see how much money we'd made the night before. Amanda wouldn't allow business to come before our morning training sessions. Good motto I suppose, but checking the bank account was the first thing I wanted to do each morning, let me tell you!

To claim your **FREE** report and DVD (valued $97) go to
www.biddingbuzz.com/book

We'd then sit down each morning and chat over a long breakfast about things we wanted to do, places we wanted to see and ways in which we wanted to expand our business. The best part of my day was opening my laptop to take a look in my PayPal account. This is our main eBay banking system (PayPal is an eBay owned company) and I'd call it my 'magic bowl'. It got that name because our cat, Burnsy, would sit by his empty food bowl every morning, staring at it, till fresh prawns magically appeared from nowhere (yes spoilt to pieces). I'd call it his magic bowl. Well, now I have my own and I love seeing the money magically appear overnight, as it does 7 days a week!

Then, around 9:30am, we would spend no more than 2 hours getting the parcels ready to post for the items we had sold, on eBay, the night before.

> ## "The best part of my day was opening my laptop to take a look in my PayPal account"

By 11.30 am we were finished and we only had to wait for the courier to collect the packages. Amanda would ask what she could do next (she was like a jumping jelly bean!). "Nothing to do." was my usual reply.

She'd ask me the same question over and over, but the thing was, I'd automated our eBay business to the point where there just wasn't that much to do. We were so excited; we had to pinch ourselves, because we couldn't believe this could really be happening for us.

We'd fill our days planning our life and what we wanted it to look like and, because we had the time to 'think', we actually achieved all the goals we set out for during that first year. Our relationship was strong and we loved spending our days together. We were relaxed and happy because we had the 'recipe' for making as many automated income streams as we felt like. There was nothing in the world that could match that feeling, for us, at the time.

> **"We were relaxed and happy because we had the 'recipe' for making as many automated income streams as we felt like"**

Making money on eBay was our dream business and the confidence and fulfillment it gave us is hard to describe. Finally we could buy anything we wanted and do what we wanted, with whom we wanted. That 'knowing' alone has been worth every second of what we've had to do to get to that point.

After about a year of enjoying our newfound freedom, Amanda became restless because she had too much time on her hands and missed the people interaction she'd experienced with her personal training business.

Apparently hanging out with me, and our Burmese cat Burnsy, wasn't exciting enough for her, 22 hours of the day!

As you know, I got what I had wished for, but in truth, I also needed a new challenge.

We realized we both wanted to create something even bigger, where it involved other people, and felt that we hadn't yet reached our full potential as entrepreneurs. Far from it as it turns out.

To claim your **FREE** report and DVD (valued $97) go to
www.biddingbuzz.com/book

We epitomized the typical ten years of hard work it took to become an overnight success. We realized through setting up our own automated eBay business, a winning system, that virtually anyone who chose to could copy and apply our winning principles and formulas, and also create the foundation of a fantastic lifestyle with unlimited income streams.

It was time to step up, step out and make a difference to peoples' lives, like we'd never done before.

This is when we turned our step-by-step system into a home-study course called 'eBay Magic'. You can find out more by visiting **www.biddingbuzz.com/book.html**

Simply enter in your details, and we'll send out a complete DVD for free, so you can get a better understanding of what is in the course.

Getting this life changing information out to people like you, was now our new found mission, or bigger purpose, and one that would truly see Amanda and myself step 'into ourselves' and finally find where we fitted in the whole grand scheme of things.

Creating and writing our 'eBay Magic' home-study course took us 10 months of working up to 100 hours a week between us. This was the biggest project we'd ever taken on, an enormous job neither of us was really prepared for, but we were on a new mission and nothing was going to hold us back. More and more, people wanted the eBay lifestyle too, and so it was a natural progression for us to want to share what we did, and how we did it, with others like you.

It had never occurred to us to keep our secrets to ourselves, it's not our nature, and after having spent in excess of $250,000 on mentors and education since we left school, we knew that to 'give back' was even more rewarding than receiving. What goes around comes around. We are blessed with an abundance mindset. There is more than enough for us all.

Amanda was now in her element sharing, teaching and motivating others, and loving every second of it. So many of our eBay Magic customers were finding financial success too, so we knew we'd made the right decision.

When you receive emails from people all over the world sharing how you've had a positive impact on their lives and how our eBay course has completely changed their financial destiny for the better, you feel all the work you've put in is so worth it.

I too had finally found my path and I now spend a lot of my time thinking of ways to expand our eBay education company and help as many people become cash and time rich, with eBay, as we can.

But enough about our story…Back to You!

Are You Ready, Willing and Able to Start Living Life on Your Terms Today?

**But enough about our story…
Back To You!
…Are You Ready, Willing and
Able To Start Living Life On
Your Terms Today?**

If setting up your own automated cash rich eBay business is right for you (we'll be getting to the nuts and bolts about that soon), then it's still going to mean rolling up your sleeves and working in your

To claim your **FREE** report and DVD (valued $97) go to
www.biddingbuzz.com/book

business initially, and it's still going to mean putting in the time up front, and it's still going to require self-management. But all these things are achievable; because we've been able to do it and so have hundreds of our customers. Now it's your turn.

The changes we had to make were fast and it will be the same for you. The biggest change we had when we started this journey, from broke to where we are today, was leaving the negative people behind.

Do you know what we mean by that?

It's hard and it's challenging, but the truth is, you end up becoming just like those you hang out with the majority of the time. That's the truth. We're not saying leave your friends and family behind; we're saying just think about who your ten closest friends are, or the ten people you spend most of your time with - we guarantee that you're income will be within five to ten percent of their average income.

> **"The truth is, you end up becoming just like those you hang out with the majority of the time"**

Think that's kind of scary? (Birds of a feather...) It was true for us so we made a point of getting around those people who made our income look pathetic! And it worked.

Our conversations became different, and so will yours, we made new friends, and so will you, we saw some old friends less and we began to think differently, as will you...and most importantly, our actions were totally different to what everyone else was doing. And yours will be too.

We began to grow and evolve into what it took to go from broke to multi-millionaires. And so will you. It was never going to happen any other way.

When we started our eBay journey, we were often laughed at by well meaning friends. Some of you have heard the story where we went to a barbeque and some old friends laughed while asking, "How's your little eBay business going these days?"

They stopped laughing when we casually told them we were turning over a minimum of $50,000 a month at the time.

"You're doing what? Can you tell us what you sell so we can do the same? Can you give us your program for free?" You know, all the usual lines.

Amanda just laughed and said "No, don't worry, you wouldn't want to know. It's not for you!"

They're not laughing anymore though. The truth is that often when people laugh at you, when they see you want to make a change, because they're embarrassed and don't want you to leave them behind. It's painful for them to see that you want something better for yourself, while they're happy to live in denial and ultimately pain.

Interestingly enough, those who laughed at us the most never asked us how we did it, or if they could invest in some education, or ask, "What did you learn or do different to get the results you have today?"

> ## "You can become whomever you want without changing who you are"

We went through a lot of changes to get where we are today. Most of you would agree that someone who progressed from a 'hands-on' carpenter to an onstage seminar presenter, teaching sophisticated eBay strategies all around the world, had to make some changes right? Old friends or family were asking,

"What are you doing? Don't you want to be one of us anymore?" Those sorts of awkward conversations were coming up more often.

The good news is you can become whomever you want without changing who you are. The most important thing you'll need to do when you've finished reading this book is to be confident, persistent and take massive action. And of course, be optimistic because you will get exactly what you expect.

If you think that this will work for you, then you're absolutely right, and if you think it won't or can't, then you're absolutely right again! It's how we think and feel about things that will cause the outcome, whether good or otherwise.

Understand that your ultimate goal may not happen for you instantly and that's okay - it's not a race - it's a matter of just being persistent and following through with the action steps that others have proven to work.

> ### "be confident, persistent and take massive action"

Become true to yourself and act on what you say you're going to do, for yourself and for your family.

We learned a great lesson, while on this journey, that we want to share with you; if you're on your journey to a better life, whatever that is for you, and you're with someone who isn't, then you must align your values with theirs (the things that are most important to you and high on your agenda) so that you can strive for the same outcome.

Otherwise it won't be easy. Your values at this point in life, right now, might be wanting to make money and wanting to become more secure.

If your business or life partner has different values to you then you must find out what they are and align them before you begin. We know for certain that if you're on the same path with the same goal in mind, the road will be much easier, smoother and far more enjoyable.

> **"The people in this world, who go on to create wealth and lifestyles to die for, have the ability to make fast decisions. They are the action takers."**

Also, practice making quick and decisive decisions, whether they are right or wrong. It doesn't matter. You'll have a result. The people in this world, who go on to create wealth and lifestyles to die for, have the ability to make fast decisions. They are the action takers. They are not procrastinators. The truth is, if you want something different, you may have to do things you've never done before… are you prepared for this?

Right now, write down at least five things that you will act on today that will change your life forever and move you closer to the outcome you truly desire for you and your family.

To claim your **FREE** report and DVD (valued $97) go to
www.biddingbuzz.com/book

"Those who reach decisions promptly and definitely know what they want, and generally get it. The leaders in every walk of life decide quickly, and firmly. That is the major reason why they are leaders. The world has the habit of making room for the man whose words and actions show that he knows where he is going."

Napoleon Hill…Think and Grow Rich

We know that if we apply our proven system, we can go online to eBay and make money instantly! For us that is true peace of mind."

Matt and Amanda Clarkson

"Success is neither magical nor mysterious. Success is the natural consequence of consistently applying basic fundamentals..."

Jim Rohn

To claim your **FREE** report and DVD (valued $97) go to
www.biddingbuzz.com/book

Chapter 6

Why There Has Never Been a Better Time To Make Unlimited Income With eBay...

Chapter 6 : Why There Has Never...

"The opportunity for making multiple streams of automated cash flow on eBay is endless, once you know what you're doing and more importantly, why you're doing it..."

Matt & Amanda Clarkson

In all our years of being in business, never have we seen an opportunity for making unlimited income streams like we have with eBay. With over 50,000 categories to choose from, and a never ending supply of buyers; all you need to do is discover all those hot, untapped markets and give the customers what they want.

> **"In all our years of being in business, never have we seen an opportunity for making unlimited income streams like we have with eBay"**

> **"Every day more than 70,000 new members flock to eBay looking to buy and sell all sorts of interesting things"**

Every day more than 70,000 new members flock to eBay looking to buy and sell all sorts of interesting things. More and more people are now turning to the Internet looking for bargains, and it's a fact that

To claim your **FREE** report and DVD (valued $97) go to
www.biddingbuzz.com/book

75% of eBay buyers earn in excess of $50,000 a year and spend an average of 2 hours on eBay each time they visit.

There is of course a bit behind the scenes but, in a nutshell, if you remember this one principle you're on your way to eBay riches if you follow all the necessary success steps. Oh yes, and here's a very important tip...

> ### "75% of eBay buyers earn in excess of $50,000 a year and spend an average of 2 hours on eBay each time they visit"

Never assume what someone will or will not buy on eBay. You have no idea what they are thinking when placing bids or buying up, so keep your assumptions to yourself!

Live by this golden rule and you will make money on eBay...simple as that.

Funnily enough, in many cases eBay shoppers buy because they are bored, want to spend money and just love the whole shopping experience. Hard to believe - but true.

You've probably heard of some crazy eBay stories yourself, where people pay astronomical amounts of money for weird or sometimes seemingly worthless items.

We have some friends in the US who divorced. As the ex-husband was preparing the house for sale, to his utter disbelief, in one of the cupboards he opened, he found 130 unopened eBay packages the ex wife had bought.

She was addicted to shopping on eBay and just loved the 'rush' of winning the auction. Amanda offered to take the parcels off his hands and resell them on eBay but I warned her not to go there!

Around 90% of eBay sellers are what we call 'dabblers' and either aren't interested or simply have no idea how to create a highly profitable business. They put things up to sell and simply 'hope for the best'.

Not a smart way to run a business if you want it to be a long-term income stream though. Because they're uneducated when it comes to knowing how to maximize profits on eBay, and simply just copy everyone else, they end up making minimal profits and often blame eBay's fees and charges for their failures. Here's where you can get the edge and cash in on other peoples laziness and ignorance!

Copying what 'the masses' do on eBay is a recipe for financial disaster, let alone the time you'll waste. There is no point in starting any business unless you know exactly how to maximize all your efforts. Why would you bother?

> **"There is no point in starting any business unless you know exactly how to maximize all your efforts"**

People are often extremely surprised at how much we invest into our 'business education', however, once they understand how much return we get, they're in awe.

Remember this. Spending money on education is an INVESTMENT and not a cost. If your education is for business purposes it should be

To claim your **FREE** report and DVD (valued $97) go to
www.biddingbuzz.com/book

tax deductable and, even if you need to go into debt for it, as long as you know you can get a great return then we call that Good Debt.

"Spending money on education is an INVESTMENT and not a cost"

Bad debt is when you spend money on things that lose value. Things like cars, TV's and impulse items that give you short-term gratification. Education can and will set you free, if you put what you learn into action! It's a fact, and one that we are so very passionate about, because we do exactly as we preach. It's no mistake that we are where we're at today; it's simply our return on investment and you can experience this too.

Once again we invested heavily in private mentoring, learning as much as we could about eBay and how to create unlimited, automated income streams. In fact, we can now create as many as we like.

"Education can and will set you free, if you put what you learn into action!"

One of the early lessons we learnt when selling on eBay was to make absolutely sure the description (title) of the item we were selling was spelt correctly. Even the slightest spelling mistake might be enough to stop bidders finding your item for sale.

Another interesting snippet of information is the majority of bids on eBay are placed between 9am and 5pm – normal working hours for most people. Little wonder many bosses won't allow their workers to log onto the eBay website!

eBay has 38 affiliated websites you can sell your products to the world from, while working in the comfort of your own home, and they have made it possible for literally anyone to make money online, virtually instantly with unstoppable traffic and hungry buyers – and best of all, you can start your own eBay business for absolutely minimal cost.

There are thousands of everyday people all over the world now making multiple streams of income through this amazing platform called eBay and, with thousands of new members joining daily, there is a never ending supply of buyers waiting to be served by you!

> **"EBay has 38 affiliated websites you can sell your products to the world from, while working in the comfort of your own home"**

Creating your own eBay business, that is highly profitable, ultimately can give you the lifestyle you've wanted for so long, if you do it right, giving you and your family peace of mind, knowing you no longer have to rely on someone else for money.

On the next page is a simple 4-step diagram of how to make money on eBay. We see eBay as the fastest, easiest and lowest risk way for you to get out of the rat race or simply to create more streams of cash flow.

> **"Creating your own eBay business, that is highly profitable, ultimately can give you the lifestyle you've wanted for so long, if you do it right, giving you and your family peace of mind"**

To claim your **FREE** report and DVD (valued $97) go to
www.biddingbuzz.com/book

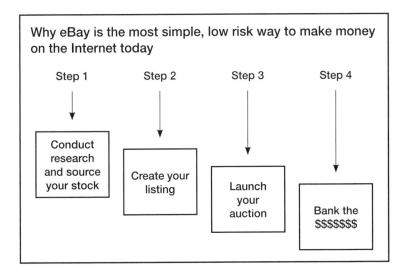

Why eBay is the most simple, low risk way to make money on the Internet today

Step 1 Step 2 Step 3 Step 4

Conduct research and source your stock

Create your listing

Launch your auction

Bank the $$$$$$$

"No matter who you are, what you're outcome is, what your background is, what your budget is, what your age is, there are literally endless ways for you to start profiting in your own eBay business…as soon as you're ready to take action, start."

Matt and Amanda Clarkson

To claim your **FREE** report and DVD (valued $97) go to
www.biddingbuzz.com/book

Chapter 7
Planning Your eBay Success...

Chapter 7 : Planning Your eBay Success...

If You Work The Proven Plan, The Proven Plan Will Work For You...

When we set out to create our full time income on eBay, we first sat down and actually discussed exactly what we wanted to achieve by having this business. I mean, in terms of time commitment, income we wanted to bring in each week and the type of selling that was best going to suit our desired outcome.

This is what we call the 'Planning' stage of your business and it's our belief that it is *by far the most important* stage of all. After all, if you don't know where you're heading, you could end up anywhere right?

So before you run off and choose your style of selling, take some time and ask yourself the following questions. You should write down your answers and then discuss each point at length with your partner, or if you're going it alone, think your answers through.

1. How much profit would you like to make on a weekly/monthly basis?

2. Would you like to sell the same items over and over, so you can automate your business, or do you like variety?

3. Exactly how much time can you put into the early stages of starting this business?

4. Are you starting on a tight budget or do you have some capital put away if you wanted to buy your own stock?

To claim your **FREE** report and DVD (valued $97) go to www.biddingbuzz.com/book

5. Do you like the idea of importing stock from places all over the world or do you want to get all your stock locally?

6. Are you prepared to hold stock in your home or storage shed and, if so, what would be the maximum size and weight you could handle comfortably?

7. Would you like to sell information products, physical products, or both?

8. Are you willing to try more than one style of eBay selling to get the financial outcome you want?

9. How much are you currently earning and would you like to replace this amount or simply create more income streams?

10. What time frame would you like this to happen in?

11. What exactly are you prepared to do to make this become your reality?

These are just a few of the many questions we discussed at length. Remember, you're about to embark on a new journey here, so getting clear up front will absolutely make it easier for you. Of course, things will change along the way, but at least you have a starting point. I call this the one page business plan and it's one that you can keep on you at all times.

When you get lost (and you will) or see too much opportunity (next shiny object) refer back to this plan and always remember your outcome. It will keep you on track.

Ok...let's go make some money on eBay!

"If you think you have the ingredients that you need, take chances, because your biggest successes will happen when you go against the tide; when you take a risk and it works"

Donald Trump

To claim your **FREE** report and DVD (valued $97) go to
www.biddingbuzz.com/book

Chapter 8
Ways You Can Start Making Maximum Profits
On eBay With Minimum Cost

Chapter 8 : 5 Ways You Can Start...

Our 'eBay Magic' home study course will show you at least 10 different ways of creating cash flow from eBay. Unfortunately, I can't get into them all here although I'd love to! You can certainly find out more later, if you want, by ordering your free DVD from our website...the web address is...

www.biddingbuzz.com/book.html

The following 5 chapters will outline some no-cost or low-cost strategies you can start with immediately, but before I get into these 5 money making eBay strategies, I've decided to give you both sides of the coin here to help you determine which of these may or may not suit you. I'm going to point out the up side and the downside of each one, so you get a clear picture of what really happens. Don't be put off however, if it was that bad or too hard we certainly wouldn't be doing it!

I'm an expert at finding 'hot untapped' markets on eBay and could spend a whole day sharing this stuff with you because no matter what you want to achieve here, there is a way that will suit you, your time frame and your budget!

Once you've got your plan worked out, it just comes down to finding out what buyers want and then getting your hands on it. The key ingredient that most successful eBay sellers have in common is the constant focus on building relationships with customers and suppliers, because we all do business with those we know, like and trust, right?

You don't have to do this face to face; it can be done via email or over the phone, however, its always better if you can meet face to face with your suppliers at some stage.

"There are many ways to get your hands on a never ending supply of stock to sell on eBay"

There are many ways to get your hands on a never ending supply of stock to sell on eBay...and once people know you're an 'eBay Magician' your biggest problem will be saying 'no.' Good problem to have, right! ;-)

At the end of the day you've just got to remember that you're dealing with everyday people like yourself and they are open to finding ways of making money too. The biggest mistake some eBay sellers make is thinking they are the ones doing people a favour when sourcing stock; when in fact, it's the other way around.

Always go in with the attitude of 'how you can make this a win-win situation' for both you and the supplier. If you keep this in mind, you will discover that 'getting your hands on a never ending supply of stock' really isn't hard at all.

The golden rule when buying stock to sell on eBay is "You make your money when you buy, not when you sell."

Just like when you buy a property...you make money going in, which means you must buy smart. Most eBay sellers have no idea about this so make sure you do your homework before you outlay any of your hard-earned money.

Moving on now, let's discover some fun and easy ways for you to start making money as soon as you've finished reading this book!

"Anybody can wish for riches, and most people do, but only a few know that a definite plan, plus a burning desire for wealth, are the only dependable means of accumulating wealth..."

Napoleon Hill

To claim your **FREE** report and DVD (valued $97) go to
www.biddingbuzz.com/book

Chapter 9
The eBay Hobbyist...

Chapter 9 : The eBay Hobbyist...

Starting out small and slowly really is the best way to get your feet wet with eBay. There's much to learn in the early days and if you're going to make any mistakes at all (don't worry, we all do!), it's best to make them in the early stages, so you don't wind up losing money or blemishing your feedback rating!

Here's where a lot of sellers start out before they work out which selling method will work best for them. A hobbyist is someone who sells on eBay for fun and wants to create an extra income stream on the side. It's perfect for those who have a job or business and need extra cash. It's also a great income generator for those who need more money but don't want to get a part time job because of time constraints.

> ## "More than 5000 Australian pensioners now rely on eBay to top up their income."

This method is also perfect for busy stay at home parents and pensioners who also need to make extra money. In fact, more than 5000 Australian pensioners now rely on eBay to top up their income. Incredible. Not only that, it's a great way for people to get 'out and about' looking for bargains and making money while having fun.

Probably the best place to start is to think about what really interests you. You may have a hobby that you really love, like 'scrap booking' or 'train collecting'. If you love your hobby, then chances are that others do too. There are many advantages to being able to market and sell items that you have a good understanding of, especially if you're truly passionate about them too!

To claim your **FREE** report and DVD (valued $97) go to
www.biddingbuzz.com/book

Also, you'll probably have a much better understanding of what the 'true' value is for your items. You can gain instant credibility, because of your in-depth knowledge and passion, which will shine through in your listings. You'll know a bargain when you see it, and be able to pick up items from other sellers who don't know what they're doing and re-sell them for a great profit.

Think about what makes you different in your field of interest. Is there a way you can illustrate, to potential bidders that buying your item will have the benefit of you as a source of knowledge to draw from later?

Are you the friendly expert, on scrap booking or train sets, people have been looking for?

Could you even write or create an information product, an E-book that you can put onto a CD, that you could sell on eBay about your hobby? Could you create a simple home made DVD teaching people how to do something?

For instance, let's say you really loved trout fishing. What if you went away fishing one weekend, and took your camcorder, and recorded every step you took that helped you catch a never-ending supply of trout?

Do you think that other fishing fanatics would like to see how you catch trout so well? You could share all your tips and tricks and make a killing with this sort of stuff. Anyway, we'll go into more depth on info products later, right now let's look at all the other possibilities to get you started.

Now, before you get all carried away and spend time and money here, make sure you know your market and have done your research and know for certain that you can make a good profit. This goes for selling any product for that matter. Being able to source products, cheaper than people can buy them for on eBay, will ensure you make a profit long term.

Now…What can you sell in the early days?

When you're first getting started with your eBay business, the best way to go about it is to choose something to sell that is…

- Of minimal Value

- Unwanted item (an unwanted gift or something!)

- It's easy to pack and post

- It's not fragile

- It's in good, clean condition

Here are a few ideas for you if you've come up blank!

- DVD's in good condition

- Fiction and non fiction books in good condition

- Old Comics

- Toys and hobbies

- CD's in good condition

- Crockery

- Consumer electronics

To claim your **FREE** report and DVD (valued $97) go to
www.biddingbuzz.com/book

- Dolls and bears

- Name brand clothing. (Must be dry cleaned)

- Motivation books, tapes, videos and DVD's

- Handbags

- Purses

- Leather goods

- Old Records

The reason it's important to start out by selling off your unwanted goods is so that you can grow your eBay feedback quickly, to gain credibility as a seller. We call it the magic 100. For some reason on eBay if you have more than 100 feedbacks, you get more credibility from potential bidders, and ultimately more money for your items.

You don't want to be 'cutting your teeth' selling items of high value, as you may lose money and, in most cases, you won't get as much for your item if you're a brand new seller as you would as a 'seasoned' seller.

There are reasons why you must grow your eBay business step by step. It's just like following a recipe…all the ingredients must be in place for the best results.

And of course, there are some things that you CANNOT sell on eBay. It's a very good idea to know about these things before you go off happily listing everything in sight! Check out the eBay Listing Policies, in the help section, and know the rules. Before you get started!

All the examples above are great ideas for you to start selling right now. This is exactly how we started our eBay business. Selling off everything in the house that wasn't nailed down! We started selling books, DVD's, tapes, Videos, CD's, wallets, shoes, handbags etc.

In the early stages of growing our eBay business, we were making a very nice income every week, just from selling things we didn't want, use or need anymore.

I'm still amazed at some of the prices we got for these items. Never assume that no one will buy what you have on offer. You do not know what other people think and feel about certain products so never try to pick the market. Let the market tell you what it wants! As you read on you'll see that I've popped a few testimonials in, just so you can see that everyday people all around the world are doing this and so can you. I can talk about it till the cows come home but I believe that if you see others can do it…then you will believe that you can too.

To claim your **FREE** report and DVD (valued $97) go to
www.biddingbuzz.com/book

Retirees, Jeff & Nancie – £1,005 in 10 days

Hi there Matt & Amanda,

Well here is the update after buying your 'eBay Magic' course. Nancie & I listened over and over again to your course; I must say we were very happy we bought. Seriously, I would highly recommend the discs and manuals, especially to new starters like us.

Well, here is also great news, we copied you guys and placed ten items from around the unit, on a 10 day Auction and sold 9 items for a total of £1,005...now I'm pretty excited about that! Wahoooooooooo!

The only Item not to sell was a 99 cent (start price) book, well 9 outa 10 ain't bad I reckon.

Thanks heaps,

Jeff & Nancie

Retirees Jeff and Nancie sent this testimonial into us after hearing about how we got started on eBay and thought they'd do the same thing. As you can see...absolutely anyone who takes action can do this too!

Downsides to being an eBay Hobbyist...

There are no real downsides, to this style of eBay business, at all except that it's hard to automate because you're selling a lot of 'one off' items. Having said this, one of our in house (Bidding Buzz trained) eBay Mentors often makes up to $1000 a week selling items she gets from the Salvation Army stores and Opportunity outlets.

She works full time with us, loves her job and the money she makes on eBay will help her to pay her first house off within 8 years instead of the usual 25.

She showed me how it only takes her less than 4 minutes to get an auction up from scratch. That's taking photos, doing the description and launching the auction. Not bad hey? This is because she sells name brand clothing and uses mostly the same descriptions. She's just become so fast at it; it's practically an automated business system she has now set up.

Another thing our in house mentor also does is, if she's going on holiday, she'll list even more items for auction and in her eBay store, so that she's not using any of her savings to fund the holiday. She uses eBay as her 'money making machine' to fund anything she wants to do.

Can you see the absolute power in this?

What do you need extra cash for and what could you be doing?

What if you were a busy stay at home parent? Could you do with some extra income on the side to help with the bills, or maybe to buy things you want, but couldn't justify buying before?

"Did you know that over 17,500 stay at home parents supplement their income using eBay as their cash cow just in Australia alone? "

Did you know that over 17,500 stay at home parents supplement their income using eBay as their cash cow just in Australia alone?

What a great idea and as you can see, stay at home mum Monique knew exactly how to take advantage of an opportunity that also awaits you right now…

Married Mum With New Born Baby Makes $2614 In First Month…And Counting

Hi Matt & Amanda,

I want to say a huge thank you! I'm loving your eBay Magic course. I thoroughly enjoy going through the manuals and CD's, and you make it so simple and straightforward to follow. I've had the material for about 4 weeks now and I've started by selling things from around the house, as you suggested. I'm up to $2,613.00 and I honestly think I'll be able to reach over $4,000 in the next few weeks. It's addictive! I love logging on and seeing whose bid, how many people are watching. I'm having great fun and making money.

A fabulous investment.

Monique. M

Another lady I know makes DVD's sharing her 'scrap booking secrets' with others who love it too. I've seen her sell up to $320 a week of these DVD's and most of that would be shear profit. What an awesome 'extra' stream of income. She only has to do the work (which is very minimal by the way) once, and hey presto…she simply just duplicates the DVDs as she sells them.

This is so smart and such a cheap way for you to make fast, easy money without too much effort. I've even seen people sell DVD's on eBay about how to clean a horse hoof and also how to change a flat tyre! I'm not joking!

Again…what hobbies are you into that you'd like to teach someone else about? What have you got to lose? All you need is a camcorder and off you go! Its really easy, cheap and a whole lot of fun.

The example on the next page shows the power of information and what people are willing to pay to learn what you know. This seller was selling a series of 'how to' DVD's on tattooing and as you can see, he or she was making great money in the process. The cost of the disk set was really the only cost after they had created the first one.

To claim your **FREE** report and DVD (valued $97) go to
www.biddingbuzz.com/book

The Ultimate Tattoo Bible: Learn How To Tattoo	℗	1 Bid Sold	$89.00
View similar active items | Sell one like this			
The Ultimate Tattoo Bible: Learn How To Tattoo	℗	1 Bid Sold	$89.00
View similar active items | Sell one like this			
The Ultimate Tattoo Bible: Learn How To Tattoo	℗	1 Bid Sold	$89.00
View similar active items | Sell one like this			
The Ultimate Tattoo Bible: Learn How To Tattoo	℗	1 Bid Sold	$89.00
View similar active items | Sell one like this			
The Ultimate Tattoo Bible: Learn How To Tattoo	℗	1 Bid Sold	$89.00
View similar active items | Sell one like this			

Here's another story…We have two customers who heard us speak about making money by simply buying people's unwanted items and re-selling them on eBay. Matt and Michelle who live on the Gold Coast followed the eBay Magic system step-by-step, sold everything around the house not nailed down and within just 3 weeks had made $2,500! (You can see their picture and testimonial on our website.)

So here's my question for you…

How would something like this make a difference to you and your situation right now? Bill and Irina…they simply sold stuff their friends and family no longer wanted, now look at them!

As you can see, there really is no downside to becoming an eBay Hobbyist. It's all about starting out selling low cost items and building from there. Of course you'll make mistakes in the early days (we did believe me!) but at least you're earning while you're learning.

I'm sure you'd agree that there's really no easier way for you to make instant income on eBay once you put your mind to it

Bill & Irina Are Making $1,600 A Month Selling Their Friend's Unwanted Things On eBay

After implementing all the eBay steps we learned from Matt & Amanda, we made $1,700 in the first three weeks Now we're making $1,600 every month selling our friends unwanted items. We're looking at expanding and getting our sales up to $10,000 a month following the eBay Magic system and with the strategies we have in place this should happen within 6 months.

Thank you Matt & Amanda.

Bill & Irina W
Sydney, Australia.

To claim your **FREE** report and DVD (valued $97) go to
www.biddingbuzz.com/book

In fact, eBay Australia suggests that every home in Australia has at least $2,200 worth of unwanted goods laying around the home that you can turn into cash right now.

What are you waiting for?

"There are no limitations to the mind except those we acknowledge....both poverty and riches are the offspring of thought...."

Napoleon Hill...Think and Grow Rich

To claim your **FREE** report and DVD (valued $97) go to
www.biddingbuzz.com/book

Chapter 10
Drop Shipping...

Chapter 10 : Drop Shipping...

Drop shipping is a great way to start out with your eBay business, if you're on a tight budget, or want to make money working on your laptop from anywhere in the world. Many people start off with a drop shipping business while 'getting their feet wet' learning the ropes, then move onto bigger better things.

Drop shipping means you deal directly with wholesalers who take care of the shipping process for you. Many sellers don't like to handle stock so this is a great way to make money without handling and shipping stock.

In a nutshell, you sell the items the drop shipper's supply and use all their photos. They hold all the stock ready for when you sell it. You then sell the products, collect the money from your buyer, and only then do you pay the drop shipper. The difference of what you sell your product for and what you pay the drop shipper is your profit. Once you pay the drop shipper, they then send the item directly to your customer and you've not handled anything except the money.

This whole process takes place before you outlay a cent of your own money!

It's common for a legitimate drop shipper to have anywhere from 5,000 to 50,000 products! Usually, they stock all the 'name brand' items which are in hot demand, which is great news for you, because when people go shopping on eBay they're quite often looking for their favourite name brands at a great bargain price.

There are literally thousands of eBay sellers who only drop ship and have very successful, lucrative businesses. This is the perfect business

To claim your **FREE** report and DVD (valued $97) go to
www.biddingbuzz.com/book

model if you do not have capital to invest in your own stock, you're a shy person and would rather run your business autonomously, or you don't feel you're ready to strike up larger deals with manufacturers and suppliers.

> ## "This is the perfect business model if you do not have capital to invest in your own stock"

Drop shipping is a fantastic way for the everyday person to be able to get into the game and sell name brand items that they otherwise might not have access to. With drop shipping you can even sell just one item at a time, if you want to start your business slowly and iron out any kinks.

Setting up a drop shipping account with overseas suppliers is very simple. There are a number of online resources that you can go to, where you can set up an account, check out the various name brand products, choose the ones you can make money selling, and then create your listing in eBay.

It's that simple...or is it?

So, let's take a closer look at how this process works. There are a few things to be aware of, before you dive in headfirst thinking that this will be the answer to all of your prayers!

One of the most important things to consider when using a drop shipper is the fact that you have lost a lot of control over your business, which can be very scary seeing as the whole eBay system relies on the 'feedback' system.

Let's dig a bit deeper.

Before you engage a 'drop shipper', to ship items to your customers, the first thing to make sure of is that the drop shipper is in fact 'legitimate.' There are many so called wholesalers in the market place that end up being 'middle men' who take profits from your pockets!

So, do your homework and make sure you're 'in business' with the right company!

The second thing I'd like to talk about is that another fact of 'drop shipping' is the low profit margins you can expect to make. The biggest profits and rewards will always come to those who source their own inventory. When using the drop shipping method, you'll have to sell a high volume of products to make a good income.

For example, we know of a young man in the US who currently turns over around $90,000 per month using the drop shipping method, and his gross income is around $10,000. He still has his own personal business expenses to cover, but I'm sure you'd agree it's a very tidy income for one month's salary, working from the spare room in your house!

We have Almost Replaced Sue's Monthly Wage Since Doing Your EBay Magic Course!

Hi There,

I just wanted to say to you both a big thank-you for everything.

I have been getting your lessons weekly now for about a month and a half and both myself and my wife Sue have been literally selling everything that isn't nailed down.

We want to move to America to emigrate there next year and we have 5 lovely children and you 2 are such an inspiration to us with the information you have been giving us.

Last month we made profit of £748- yes profit, after everything was taken off completely, now that is just short of Sue's wages for the month and this month so far, September, we have sold over £322 worth of products we have sourced using Salehoo. We have our first pallet load of goods arriving on Monday and are so exited about it. Next year we want to come to one of your workshops in Australia and all I can say is, thank God I got to see you at a seminar Matt & Amanda.

Thank you both again.
Frank, Sue and the kids of course. Scotland

The typical margin for sellers using this method is anything from 2% -20%. (There about) At the end of the day this number can vary quite a bit, and some sellers do make a higher margin. All you've got to remember is that you make your money going in, so buy smart.

Don't take notice of what the drop shippers say the 'retail' price is, as you won't sell it for full retail on eBay. That's a fact of life when it comes to selling on this platform.

You'll need to do your due diligence to find out exactly what you'll make back in profit for the effort you put in. Remember, time is money.

Here are some facts you should know about drop shipping and dealing with manufactures/wholesalers that may be useful when you begin your research.

- Search engines are the domain of the 'middle man'. You'll more than likely not have much luck finding a legitimate wholesaler using this method.

- Most real wholesalers do not market to home-based businesses. They usually deal directly with retail businesses. Yes, eBay is classed as a home-based business.

- Plenty of wholesalers are happy to work with home-based businesses; however you must develop great business relationships. This is where your 'social' skills will come into practice!

- You need to go straight to the source. By this I mean the manufacturer of the products, and they will know who the real wholesalers are.

- The brand name on the box is not always the name of the manufacturer.

- Somewhere on the product's packaging, you'll almost always find the manufacturer. Keep your eyes peeled. Look at the product, the user manual and the instructions for information.

- Don't give up if you get a few 'no's'. Remember…each 'no' is one step closer to the 'yes' you want!

One of the best and most legitimate drop shipping companies that we recommend, and also eBay recommends, is World Wide Brands. If you'd like to investigate the various options and compare drop-shipping companies, you can find the top options that we would recommend at…

www.Biddingbuzz.com.au/products.html

> **"Don't give up if you get a few 'no's'. Remember…each 'no' is one step closer to the 'yes' you want! "**

World Wide Brands, now known as One Source, is eBay recommended and a place where you'll find legitimate wholesalers who are happy to do business with eBay sellers. They boast the Worlds largest database of ecommerce wholesalers and the below picture is what the site looks like. It is user friendly and you can see they offer a whole range of ways you can get your hands on stock.

You can buy large volumes of stock, you can buy small amounts of stock, you can buy liquidated stock, and they even have an area where you can conduct market research before you jump in and buy anything.

At a recent eBay event we attended, a spokesperson for World Wide Brands shared that they had actually contacted more than 60,000 suppliers just to get 5,000 brand name suppliers on their books. As you can see, it takes massive amounts of work and a long time to build good business relationships with big name companies.

Some US wholesalers will expect you to have a USA tax ID number, which means you need to have a registered company in the USA to use them.

This can be overcome simply by registering a business in either Nevada or Delaware via the Internet and there are many websites on the Internet that can help you here.

This is an extremely normal process and is possible for anyone willing to begin trading in the US market on a larger scale. At the end of the day, if you want to run a serious eBay business you're going to have to do a few things to make yourself legitimate. Real wholesalers will expect you to go through this process so be prepared for it.

The best way to go is to just get on the phone and call the person you'll be dealing with and get their help with this process. You will find that they're more than willing to help you.

With some brand name items you may be required to get a 'reseller license'. This, too, can be an advantage if you happen to find a great new brand that isn't currently being sold in your country.

Because there are a lot more buyers on eBay than there are sellers, your hard work can pay off very handsomely, if you carry out the necessary research. A lot of sellers simply 'give up' when they're required to set their business up properly, instead of just working through the simple steps necessary.

When you get to this level of business, it really forces you to focus and answer the question…
"What do my buyers want?"

Work that out, supply it, and you're home free.

And here's how you do it, step by step.

STEP 1:
Conduct your research to find a hot market on eBay. Use research tools of your choice and check completed listings for that same item.

STEP 2:
Set up your account with your chosen drop shipping company. Get on the phone and ask them to help you if you need to. They are all looking for new business so they're more than happy to speak with you directly.

STEP 3:
Find the hot in demand products and make sure they're at a price which allows you to still make a profit. Never buy products until you know for sure you'll make money. By doing your research in step two, you'll have the answers you need.

STEP 4:

Copy the text and photos from the supplier to add to your listings. Depending on the company, this will come either in the form of a CD with all of the products listed; it could be online and you can copy and paste the HTML code into your listing; or it might come in a CFU file which allows you to upload the whole range of products to your eBay store within minutes.

(From the information above you can see that if you want to drop ship in bulk, then you either need more advanced listing skills, or you may need to pay someone to do that work for you.)

Again, if in doubt call the drop-shipper for extra help.

STEP 5:

List the items in your store and drive traffic to your eBay Store by using Buy It Now auctions, eBay Featured marketing options, like Featured Plus, Featured Home page, or any of the more advanced marketing strategies you'll learn later in this program.

STEP 6:

Make the sale through your store and process the transaction into your own account.

STEP 7:

Order the item from your drop-shipping supplier, who will then send it directly to your customer, once you've sent them the customer details and the money for the item.

STEP 8:

Follow up the process by keeping in touch with the customer until they receive the product. Leave feedback for your customer once you've received positive feedback from them.

STEP 9:

Refine your listings to improve the bidding prices and increase sales. If possible, begin to eliminate non-selling products and focus on your hottest selling items. Continual market research will help you with this process.

> **"Never treat your eBay business like a hobby unless you only want to make very minimal income. A true business that is profitable, and continues to grow and expand, takes work and dedication, and most of all, total belief in your own abilities to make it happen"**

STEP 10:

Email market to your growing database of customers to increase backend sales. Cross promote different items that are relative to the customer. Remember, it's always easier to sell to an existing customer than it is to gain new ones. Repeat the whole process till you reach your goals.

Most importantly, never be discouraged when you're going through this process of finding the right wholesaler or drop-shipper that's best for you. Just like any other 'bricks and mortar' business, an eBay business does require some initial work and due diligence on your part.

Never treat your eBay business like a hobby unless you only want to make very minimal income. A true business that is profitable, and continues to grow and expand, takes work and dedication, and most of all, total belief in your own abilities to make it happen.

Always remember, there are plenty of other people just like you who have done all the steps required to become successful on eBay.

Let's take a look at the few 'downsides' of running a drop shipping business on eBay...

There are a couple of downsides to drop shipping in our opinion. Firstly, you're relying on the wholesaler to have the stock you sell at hand, plus, get the parcels out to your customers, which means you don't have total control over your business. And of course, as you well know, eBay is built on the 'feedback' system. Also, many people are using the same drop shippers and selling the same goods so you're up against a lot of sellers with the same items.

Another thing we notice is that most eBay sellers who have a drop shipping business (the ones who don't know better) wouldn't think to take their own photos of the products, they simply use the 'stock images' like everyone else. What this means is, you all look the same to the buyer and it can be 'pot luck' as to who gets the sale.

Also, you need to be careful that even if the drop shipper says he has plenty of stock, and then they don't once you've sold something, then this is your problem and your reputation on the line. This can happen especially around busy periods of the year like Christmas and Easter time. So be careful here.

At the end of the day if you sell stock that you can't fulfill, your customers won't be happy and it's your responsibility to keep them happy.

Lastly, I want you to note that these are our thoughts and opinions only and we don't mean to turn you off drop shipping. I promised I'd give you 'the good, the bad and the ugly' and all I hope is that you take precautions, because we want you to be super successful with your eBay business too.

Below are examples of two legitimate drop shipping companies that many of our members are using to make money with on eBay.

Salehoo and you can also find them at www.Biddingbuzz.com.au/products.html

You will find everything you need to know here.

Factory Fast is another Australian company that will drop ship for you or you can buy wholesale products if you prefer. They also sell directly to the consumer market.

OK, just to clarify the process once more, below is the exact sequence of how drop shipping can work for you.

- You deal directly with legitimate, brand name wholesalers

- You list the item for sale on eBay

- The customer buys the item and you bank the money

- You pay the wholesaler and they then ship the item directly to your customer

- The difference between the wholesale price and your selling price is your profit

To claim your **FREE** report and DVD (valued $97) go to
www.biddingbuzz.com/book

- You never have to handle the item

- Perfect if you want to sit at your laptop and travel the world

"The big idea is to fall in love with your customers...
Not your product or service.
Do this right, and your customers will become your evangelists and grow your business via word of mouth beyond your wildest dreams..."

Matt and Amanda Clarkson

"People are like stained-glass windows. They sparkle and shine when the sun is out, but when the darkness sets in, their true beauty is revealed only if there is a light from within."

Elizabeth Kubler Ross

To claim your **FREE** report and DVD (valued $97) go to
www.biddingbuzz.com/book

Chapter 11

un An eBay Consignment Business And Sell
Other People's Goods For Them...

If you're the type of person who'd love to have a never ending supply of products to sell on eBay, but don't want to go through the continuous task of sourcing them, then running an eBay consignment business could be the way to go for you!

Selling on consignment means that you sell other peoples' products or services for them if they don't know how to, or don't want to. You, the seller would take the pictures of the item, list on eBay in the correct category, select the correct listing type, sell the item and ship it. After this, you would share up the profits with the owner of the stock minus the eBay fees and charges.

This is how a lot of people run their business, however there are no hard and fast rules unless you have a franchise system. It comes down to how you run your business and the agreement both you and the owner of the stock have at the time.

"Here's a way you can make hundreds or thousands of dollars each week with very little cost or risk involved"

Here's a way you can make hundreds or thousands of dollars each week with very little cost or risk involved.

Not only that, you can also decide to only accept items at a minimum value so that you're not wasting your time with people that just bring you un-sellable junk. For example, you may only take items that have a minimum value of at least $50 to make it worth your while.

To claim your **FREE** report and DVD (valued $97) go to www.biddingbuzz.com/book

It's our belief that this is one of the easiest and most profitable ways of running an eBay business if you can get the right deals and partnerships. We also know, from our own experience, that once you become known as a smart, educated and successful eBay seller that deals come to you thick and fast. Again, and from our experience, with this style of business, your biggest problem will be turning customers away!

> **"It's our belief that this is one of the easiest and most profitable ways of running an eBay business if you can get the right deals and partnerships"**

> **"With this style of business, your biggest problem will be turning customers away!"**

Because running a consignment business is a very popular choice amongst our eBay Magic members, we have gone into great detail about this method of selling and exactly how to go about getting a never ending supply of products to sell. We've even supplied different ads you can copy and agreements you can use if this is for you. We even tell you how to approach the store owners and what to say.

There are so many retail businesses out there that have surplus stock they can't move - it's unbelievable! In most cases, traditional 'bricks and mortar' business owners are too tired or too busy to even bother about learning how to sell on eBay, so they're very, very open to speaking with successful and reputable eBay sellers like you. It's all about how you 'handle yourself' during the process.

If you do this right, you'll have a never-ending supply of stock to sell on eBay and just by way of 'word of mouth' before long, you'll be in hot demand.

You may want to choose a specific category or product that you'd like to market and sell, or you can take on a large variety of products. It all depends on how comfortable you are researching and knowing the market you're about to sell into.

Always keep this in mind…when you're choosing products you'd like to sell on consignment ongoing, ask yourself if it's going to be easy to automate. You don't want to create too much hard work. Try to get deals where you're selling a 'cluster' of products in the one category and things you may be able to get hold of again and again.

> **"If you do this right, you'll have a never-ending supply of stock to sell on eBay and just by way of 'word of mouth' before long, you'll be in hot demand."**

Some people may think this is impossible, but it's not. We speak to business owners all the time who have access to name brand products that they can get on an ongoing basis. Of course, you may have to wait till end of season or sales to get your stock, but it could be very worthwhile for you. And while there might be variations on the products, some of the process can definitely be automated.

Whichever way you choose to go, running a consignment business on eBay can be a very rewarding and profitable choice.

Let's explore in depth, exactly how you'd go about starting and running your eBay consignment business, starting right now. We'll look at a couple of different ideas.

Called one of the "13 Hot Businesses for 2005" by Entrepreneurs magazine, eBay consignment stores are popping up everywhere.

The iSold It drop off store franchise specifies the items for on-line sale

 The iSold It franchise can help clients in selling items that have an expected value of $30 or more on eBay, with weight below 70 kg and measure less than 130 inches in length and girth combined. The business services firm can sell items including cameras and video recorders, antiques and collectables, electronics and phones, appliances and furniture, sports equipment, vehicle parts and musical instruments.

The drop off store takes pride in selling valuable large items on eBay. Clients need not bring the large items to the iSold It stores. Just some pictures and a description about the item will do. Customers should provide over 10 photos of the item, out of which iSold It will use up to eight pictures in eBay listing. Photographs should reveal any design detail, manufacturer name, special markings, etc. The photos should also provide a view of any significant scratches, dents, tears, stains or other flaws in the item to give a fair presentation on eBay.

After receiving the necessary information and photographs from the customer, iSold It will confirm the appropriateness of the item for sale on eBay. The business services firm will create a listing and post the item on eBay.

23-Jan-2008

At the moment, franchised 'drop off stores' are leading the way. The number one ranked consignment franchise in America, "iSold It", currently boasts 900 stores under contract and is planning a further 3000 to open in all 50 states in the USA. There is a new iSold It consignment store opening every second day, with a minimum starting cost of US$85,000, plus working capital!

Another US giant in the consignment franchise stores is a company called"Auction Drop". In 2005 they started with only a few stores and have now teamed up with UPS (United Parcel Services), which owns a whopping 3400 stores. This means, people can now drop off their 'unwanted goods for sale' at any of the 3400 UPS stores.

"The downsides of this type of business are very, very minimal"

Another US company PostNet, which has 500 franchises that offer copying and shipping services, has just added auction services.

So, as you can see, the consignment business is absolutely booming in the US and will no doubt take off around the world.

It's only a matter of time before you could start seeing franchised Drop Off Stores popping up in your neighborhood! While many of the consignment or drop off stores in America are independently owned, many are choosing to go with one of the leading franchises because of the branding power.

Of course, while being part of a franchise has many benefits, you can always start at home, and then as you grow bigger, look at moving into more suitable premises. Remember, you're responsible for the stock you're holding that belongs to other people, so make sure you have the appropriate paper work, insurances and security in place.

You can choose between selling everyday items for friends, family and people you meet or you can approach businesses and help them move surplus stock or sale stock. You will need to make sure you are time managed and detailed with this type of business as you may be dealing with a few suppliers. This isn't hard but it definitely is very important for your success.

Right now is the best time to help these retailers out, with all that's happening in the economy. If you know what you're doing, they are

To claim your **FREE** report and DVD (valued $97) go to
www.biddingbuzz.com/book

more than happy to chat with you and we know of amazing deals some of our eBay Magic customers are putting together right now!

My advice is to hold the stock if you can, so you're in control. You may even come to an agreement where you're able to buy the stock very cheaply and the retailer continues to supply you as needed. There's a variety of things you can do here! I'm excited just typing this!

We have approached name brand stores and offered our services as a test and the response was overwhelming. The retailers often don't have the time or desire to learn how to sell on eBay properly but YOU could so here's a perfect low cost or no cost way for you to start today.

Let's take a look to see if there are any downsides to this…

The downsides of this type of business are very, very minimal and this is why I like it so much.

One downside to this method is if you sell an item for someone and they then change their mind. You must make sure that what you're selling is going to go to the winning buyer or you will face negative feedback. Don't ever forget that this is your responsibility so make sure you're careful who you deal with.

Also, it's not as easy to automate this type of business, as you'll be selling 'one off' items unless you move into a 'category' and can get your hands on the same items over and over again.

Lastly, if you're not a 'people' person and you don't like being organized then forget it! You will not like this type of eBay business so don't even go there in my opinion ;-)

So you can see I haven't really come up with many downsides, so if you could see yourself selling other peoples' things for them ongoing, then go for it!

To finish up here, below is an outline of some of the benefits of selling other peoples things on eBay.

- Once you become known as an eBay business, people will literally hound you to list and sell their products for them and share in the profits.

- There are endless opportunities in the market place for selling other peoples goods on a consignment basis. You can sell for the general public, go for the retail market or even wholesalers.

It's up to you and again you're only limited by your own thoughts and beliefs here.

- It's easy, and your business will very quickly spread via word of mouth. Before long you won't be 'looking' for business…the business will come to you.

- It's perfect if you're on a tight budget and want to start slowly while building your business.

- You can run this business from home, purchase a drop off franchise or start your own drop off store in your local town.

- If you're a 'people' person this business will be perfect for you.

To claim your **FREE** report and DVD (valued $97) go to
www.biddingbuzz.com/book

> "It's perfect if you're on a tight budget
> and want to start slowly while building
> your business"

"Within each of us lies the power of our consent to health and sickness, to riches and poverty, to freedom and to slavery. It is we who control these, and not another."

Richard Bach

Chapter 12

ow To Buy Cheap Items From eBay And
Sell Them For Big Profits

Chapter 12 : eBay Arbitrage...

Have you ever heard of the term Arbitrage?

Arbitrage is the term used traditionally in the financial world where people purchase and sell the same securities, commodities, or currencies, in different markets to profit from unequal prices.

That's the fancy term but what does it all have to do with eBay?

You can actually run a full time, very profitable business, just by buying items on eBay, from sellers who have no real understanding of what they're doing. You then simply re-list them on eBay and sell them at a higher price.

So let's dig a little deeper and see how you can use this strategy...

Here's a good example for you. There's a seller in the US who runs a full time eBay business exclusively selling calculators. He sources 100% of his stock from other sellers on eBay who cannot spell the word 'calculator' properly. He buys a lot of stock very cheap because of this and simply re-sells it at higher prices. Much higher in fact.

We know of many sellers doing this type of business right now because it's easy and you have a never-ending supply of products to sell.

> **"You can actually run a full time, very profitable business, just by buying items on eBay, from sellers who have no real understanding of what they're doing"**

Some of the mistakes these other uneducated sellers are making are…

- They are listing their products in the wrong category

- They misspell the keywords in their auction listing titles

- They end their auctions at a time when less buyers are looking

- Their listings are poorly written with no benefits outlined

- They take and upload appalling photos so the buyer cannot see exactly what they're purchasing

- They are not using Gallery Images in their listings

- Their buying terms and conditions are unclear to the buyer

- They don't come across as trustworthy and knowledgeable

- Their feedback rating is either very poor or very low

- And so on…

Think about how you might take advantage of this exciting information and create an eBay arbitrage business, just like in the example above.

So firstly how would you go about finding these listings that aren't listed correctly?

STEP 1: Decide on your niche market by finding out what's hot and what's not on eBay.

STEP 2: Scour the current listings to find the ones that are either getting no bids, or extremely low bids, or listings without a Gallery Image (a picture of the item shown beside the listing in the eBay search results) and start to pick off the bargains that you know you can make money from (Note: Don't buy anything unless you know for sure that you can relist it, sell it, and make a good profit).

STEP 3: Go to this website www.fatfingers.com where you'll find a search tool that specialises in finding misspelled search terms used on eBay. You can pick from any of the eBay websites around the world, to get even more targeted information.

For example, sticking to our 'calculator' story, here's a list of the misspelled words we found in this category alone...

calvulator, valculator, calxulator, xalculator, calculstor, cslculator, calculatpr, calculatir, calcilator, calcylator, calculayor, calcularor, calculitor, cilculator, calcwlator, calculatoo, calculattr, calculaaor, calculltor, calcuuator, calcclator, callulator, caaculator, cclculator, calculatorr, calculatoor, calculattor, calculaator, calcullator, calcuulator, calcculator, callculator, caalculator, ccalculator, calculatro, calculaotr, calcultaor, calcualtor, calcluator, caluclator, caclulator, claculator, aclculator, calculato, calculatr, calculaor, calcultor, calcuator, calclator, calulator, caculator, clculator, alculator

As you can see there are many eBay sellers and buyers that have trouble typing in the correct spelling of this particular word. Here's just a sample of a few listings we found with incorrect spelling in the Listing Title. We have circled the incorrect words for you. What you don't see here is that none of them have any bids.

To claim your **FREE** report and DVD (valued $97) go to
www.biddingbuzz.com/book

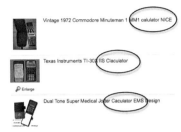

What you'd then do is click on each of the listings, have a look at the descriptions, shipping policies and the feedback. From the information you've gathered, you would soon be able to know a good deal at a glance and be able to pick the cherries from the bad listings.

Running an arbitrage business is a little bit like panning for gold. Initially you'll be putting in long research hours, but when you find the gems, you can make extremely good returns.

Another plus for running this type of business is that you'll be able to source 100% of your stock on eBay. With millions of live listings on any given day, you can practically pick up bargains all day long!

In fact, one of our eBay Mentors also uses this method for making big money on eBay. She shops at Op shops and she also uses Arbitrage to score amazing bargains! I've seen her buy Joey True Religion jeans from an eBay seller, who didn't know what she was doing, for $20 and then resell them for a whopping $120! That's $100 gross profit. Not bad for about fifteen minutes work eh?

Don't forget there are plenty of other auction sites you can visit to get your stock from. There are literally thousands of sellers all around the world trying to sell items with absolutely no idea how to do it right. Here's your chance to learn the ropes, do it the right way from the beginning and profit big time. Go for it!

Are there any downsides to running this type of eBay business?

The only real downside of this business is that it may take a while to stock up on goodies to re-sell, but that's certainly no reason not to get started right away. You can start right this minute!

One thing to mention is that you don't just have to find stock that has been spelt incorrectly. There are still many sellers who have spelt their key listing title words correctly but still don't have the best listings and make many of the other mistakes shown above.

We met a lady in America who created a whole business on eBay by simply buying women's brand name business suits from other sellers and then resold the suits back onto eBay with a better listing and using many of the listing strategies we speak about in our eBay Magic program.

This lady now works from home and makes on average US $120,000 and has more time and freedom to spend her days as she chooses.

Arbitrage isn't just limited to other auction websites either. There are many classified websites out there such as Craigslist and the Trading Post, where you can grab a bargain and then resell it onto eBay.

One of the great bonuses of selling on eBay is they just have so much traffic or potential bidders.

On the other hand, many of these smaller sites really just don't get that much internet traffic compared to eBay. What this means is that when people try to sell their item on another website, they really are not able to maximize their selling potential, simply because not enough people will see their offering.

Over all, this is a fantastic strategy where you can get started right now for very little financial outlay. Of course, it will require you to learn the ropes before you can go out and attempt to do this effectively, but with minimal effort that challenge can be overcome very quickly.

"Whatever we think about and thank about we bring about..."

Dr. John Demartini

Chapter 13
Sell Your Own Information Products

Chapter 13 : Sell Your Own Information...

We know of many eBay sellers who have a talent or a hobby and have been able to turn those skills into big profits by showing other people how to do the same.

For instance, we know of a lady who created a DVD on how to design and make beautiful hair bows in the USA and was selling them on eBay for $99.00 She was selling between 1-2 a day which means she was selling at least $700 a week worth of those DVD's. Her profits would have been over 80% if not more.

The beautiful thing about creating and selling your own information products is the high profit margins you can make and how simple this business is to automate.

It doesn't have to be 'high tech' or anything like that, you can simply use your home video or recorder to create these products.

The other great thing about this method of selling is the fact that you won't have much competition, which is fantastic. You can run it from anywhere in the world and it's just too easy.

We could go on for hours here, with examples of what other sellers are doing successfully, but Matt's telling me to get a move on. During our 3-day eBay Magic live workshop we spend at least 2 hours just on this one topic! And that's not enough time either!

I don't really see any downside to this type of eBay business, and in fact, if you're creative and have something that others want to know about you can create a very lucrative business indeed.

To claim your **FREE** report and DVD (valued $97) go to
www.biddingbuzz.com/book

Your own products could be:

- Digital products, such as eBooks and audio downloads. These types of products are ideal but to comply with eBay rules they must delivered in a physical format, e.g. on a CD ROM.

- Physical products, such as DVDs and CDs. By creating your own hard products you have the opportunity to dominate your chosen category. As an example, a lighting expert created his own DVD and in one January, a bad month for selling anything usually, in a 15-day period he had sales of more than $7500 selling his own DVD. And a DVD is inexpensive to ship anywhere in the world!

- Products created from your own expertise. Open up your mind and think about what you are good at that others would like to know about.

It could be making Australia's best chocolate biscuits or grooming your dog. Absolutely anything people have an interest in buying.

- A restaurant sells dinners for two on eBay. Others sell bed and breakfast accommodation and another ad we noted with great interest was for a complete wedding ceremony - $2,500 for 50 people. An interesting side to some of these sales is that in some cases the purchase will never be taken up even though it's been paid for. Someone may buy a dinner for friends who for various reasons will never take up the offer.

- Services. If you're selling a service, eBay has dedicated service sites where you can advertise for far less than the cost of a newspaper ad. One holistic massage business uses eBay to sell gift certificates and this is only one example of many I'd like to share with you.

The next few examples show just how profitable information products can be…

Public Domain – You can use a variety of information that falls into the Public Domain after the copyright period ends. You can create a number of different products using Public Domain works like audio files, magazine clippings, films or even images.

What you need to take away from this chapter is that making money on eBay has many forms and it's possible to actually merge more than one of these strategies together. We might sell an information product to generate interest in what we have to offer, or we might include an information product in a physical product we have to sell, and the information product creates massive value.

Not only that, it allows us to stand out from the crowd and be seen as the expert in our chosen field.

To claim your **FREE** report and DVD (valued $97) go to
www.biddingbuzz.com/book

This gives the bidders extra reassurance in knowing that they are making the right choice bidding with us, and therefore they might even bid the auction up higher to win the item.

"Train yourself to be an idea's magician. Once you get started it's hard to stop because you can't stop seeing opportunity! Let me warn you though – it becomes addictive!"

Matt and Amanda Clarkson

"Every great teacher who has ever walked the planet has told you that life was meant to be abundant...."

James Ray

"If you love what you do, you are going to work harder, and everything is going to come easier. To be successful, you need to love what you do. "

Donald Trump

Chapter 14
Bringing It All Together...

Chapter 14 : Bringing It All Together...

"Most of us have never allowed ourselves to want what we truly want, because we can't see how it's going to manifest."

Jack Canfield

Building a long-term, profitable eBay business takes precise planning just as building a high-rise building does. It's all about building a strong foundation so that the business continues to grow and stay profitable for the long term. Remember, you are building an asset here, so it's important to follow every success step in order for this to become your reality.

Finding a never-ending supply of items to sell on eBay is the easy part. Creating something of value though takes time, a lot of thinking and most importantly, the right kind of action.

Don't worry though, because we've made this part easy for you.

We've spent our time, money and effort putting together a proven, easy system so that you won't have to and you'll save up to 3-5 years of stuffing around trying to work it out for yourself. What a relief, eh?

"Building a long-term, profitable eBay business takes precise planning just as building a high-rise building does."

To claim your **FREE** report and DVD (valued $97) go to
www.biddingbuzz.com/book

We show you exactly, step-by-step, how to do this so that you can avoid all the painful and expensive mistakes we've made along the way. After all, who's got time to 're-invent the wheel' as they say? You will need a notepad, pen and a highlighter for the final chapters so that you can take notes, highlight your action steps and begin to prepare your own 'blueprint' to eBay profits.

Even though we can't give this process justice in the last few chapters, we'll do our best, however, if you can't wait for all the answers you can certainly find out more by going to our website and asking for some free information.

> **"We show you exactly, step-by-step, how to do this so that you can avoid all the painful and expensive mistakes we've made along the way"**

There is a lot to cover here and when we do our three day eBay Magic workshop, 'Zero to a Million & Beyond on eBay", we spend three full days covering this live. You see, it's not just about selling stuff on eBay with no real plan...it's about building an asset of real value because we believe this is what you want, right?

Anyway, let's get into it now because this is where we want to show you how to bring all this new found knowledge and information together, then break it down into 'bite' sizes so that it all makes perfect sense for you and you can get started immediately!

Are you getting excited yet?

Over the next few chapters we've broken down our 'eBay blueprint for big profits' formula, which saw us go from zero to millionaires in under two years, selling everyday items on eBay. Now we want to show you how to achieve the same, or any amount that you desire. Of course, you have to believe it can happen for you too, so imagine the amount of money that you'd like to make each week or month, write it down, highlight it, see and feel it as though you already have it right now with gratitude, and then follow the following steps to untold eBay riches. Whatever that means for you.

Remember...know your outcome (reasons for doing this) and stick to the plan...

To claim your **FREE** report and DVD (valued $97) go to
www.biddingbuzz.com/book

"At the end of your life, you will never regret not having passed one more test, not winning one more verdict, or not closing one more deal. You will regret time not spent with a husband, a friend, a child, or a parent. "

Barbara Bush

Chapter 15

our 7 Easy Steps To Personal Success And
Big eBay Profits

Chapter 15 : Yours 7 Easy Steps To...

Step 1: Whatever You Think About Most ...You Will Experience.

"The key here is to get your headspace and mindset right. Because you will experience exactly what you expect in life. So right from the very beginning, plan to settle for nothing less than success. That's financial and personal success whatever that means for you. Be very clear, precise and focused. You'll be amazed at how powerful your thoughts truly are..."

Amanda Clarkson

"Here's the problem...most people are thinking about what they don't want, and they're wondering why it shows up over and over again."

John Assaraf.

Right now you're probably thinking 'just give me your money making secrets so I can get on with it!' Well, hold your horses for a moment because they're coming right up, but before we get to the 'nuts and bolts of making money' there are a couple of things we must talk about, you and me...

If you want wealth and personal success to become part of your life you must get your thinking and mindset right. Yes, I know we've already covered a lot of this in the beginning of the book but I just want to drive home to you the importance of having a positive attitude and being an action taker, because here's where most people fall off the wagon.

> ## "If you want wealth and personal success to become part of your life you must get your thinking and mindset right"

You must now open your mind and expect success. If you keep an open mind it will happen for you. You know the power of positive thinking. Stay away from negative people and do whatever it takes to make this happen. There has never been a better time to be making money on the Internet than right now so you may have to keep some of your plans to yourself so that others can't sabotage you.

> ## "Because here's where most people fall off the wagon"

The number one reason why we've been able to create massive success in our personal and financial life is because everyday we spend at least one hour listening to 'personal development' DVDs. We work on our 'headspace' so that we can mentally keep up with our own growth. And of course we take massive action in the right direction every single day.

> **"The number one reason why we've been able to create massive success in our personal and financial life is because everyday we spend at least one hour listening to 'personal development' DVDs"**

> **"You see, the only reason why so many people never experience what they truly desire in life is because they don't grow and develop their mindset"**

Just wishing and hoping for a free ride won't make you rich either. You're dreaming if you believe this.

You see, the only reason why so many people never experience what they truly desire in life is because they don't grow and develop their mindset. If you don't change your mindset and begin to think differently than you do now, your bank balance or your lifestyle will not change either. It's a fact.

You know the old saying...the definition of insanity is doing the same thing day in, day out, and expecting a different result. It's not going to happen sunshine.

So what are you prepared to do today to get a different result? Write it down and highlight it now.

To claim your **FREE** report and DVD (valued $97) go to
www.biddingbuzz.com/book

'Your future has nothing to do with your past.'

The truth is that we never really understood the power of this until after one whole year of doing everything we needed to do to change our thinking, which saw us get results beyond our wildest dreams. And everyone else's too. Our choice of mentors for this ranged from Tony Robbins to Dr John Demartini, Mark Sneddon, Bob Proctor, The Secret, Mal Emery, Robert Kyosiaki, Dale Carnegi, Napoleon Hill and many others.

We read tons of books, listened to countless DVDs, attended a heap of seminars and made the necessary changes to become who we are today. Successful and happy.

"Our job is not to figure out the how. The how will show up out of a commitment and belief in the what."
Jack Canfield...The Secret

In this case, the 'how' is eBay and the 'what' is your burning reason. What is your burning reason? Write it down and highlight it. Your reason is why you get up every morning and do whatever it will take to get your outcome.

Do you want more money? Why? Do you want more time? Why? Do you want better health? Why? Do you want more love? Why? Do you want to love yourself more? Why? These are some examples of what your reasons may be. Write them down and highlight them now.

Less than 5% of sellers on eBay truly understand how to create a real and profitable eBay business and take it seriously. It's not their fault, they just don't know any better. But you do so you'll have the edge, right?

If you were to get real serious, work on your mindset and get totally focused about your outcome, what could you achieve on eBay? Can you visualize and feel the opportunity available here from what we've shared so far? If so, let's move on…

Step 2 : It's All About Getting Your eBay Goggles On And Seeing Product Sourcing Opportunities Everywhere!

The million dollar question…"What am I going to sell on eBay & where do I get it?"This would be our most asked question of all when people ask us about how to make money on eBay.

Our simple answer to this is,"If you ask better questions you'll get better answers."

> ### "Is there a proven system I can easily follow and how can I fast track this process without painful, costly mistakes?"

Perhaps a better question may be, "How do I make real money on eBay, like the smart 2% of sellers do? Is there a proven system I can easily follow and how can I fast track this process without painful, costly mistakes?"

You see, it's all about having all of the pieces of the jigsaw puzzle in your hands so you know without a doubt that you can do this all by yourself. It's like having your very own treasure map. Once you know how to find a never-ending supply of things to sell on eBay, and do it right, so you make a lot of money, all your fears and hesitations fly out the window. And you can do it again and again.

To claim your **FREE** report and DVD (valued $97) go to
www.biddingbuzz.com/book

Can you see how this makes sense once you know how?

Mastering all the techniques will ensure you never run out of ideas and things to sell.

Probably one the most *frustrating* and *difficult* tasks as an eBay seller, is the ongoing and time consuming task of sourcing a regular supply of hot selling items to sell through your eBay business. Don't despair, you're not alone, because each and every eBay seller has at one stage had the same hurdles while trying to grow their business.

In the early stages of most eBay businesses, everyday people, just like you, generally start out by selling *unwanted items* they have sitting around the home that are no longer wanted, needed or used. But of course eventually you'll want to grow your business and automate it as much as you can.

What happens in a lot of cases, (including our own) is that you start out by selling off these unwanted items, and once you start selling and making money on just about everything you list on eBay, all of a sudden you find yourself 'hooked'. Next thing, you're stalking around the house in search for anything that isn't nailed down that you can list and sell for a profit!

> **"It's like having your very own treasure map. Once you know how to find a never-ending supply of things to sell on eBay, and do it right, so you make a lot of money, all your fears and hesitations fly out the window. And you can do it again and again"**

But as can be expected, you soon run out of 'things' to sell from around the house. Once you've collected and sold everything you could get your hands on from your friends and neighbours, you're left with the job of sourcing an on-going supply of merchandise.

Well, the *good news* is, there are quite a few ways that you can go about finding never ending supplies of product to sell in your eBay business. But before we get into this, there are a couple of steps you'll first need to put into place.

The *first* and most important step is to **develop your 'Product Finding Mindset'**. This simply means that if you want to be 'switched on' to what's hot on eBay, there are a few tips and tricks you can develop that will give you a great head start.

First of all, when you're going through the process of deciding what types of products you'd like to sell on eBay, you have to put yourself into the consumers' mindset to find out exactly what it is that they want or need to buy. Here are four steps to help you.

Open Minded Ideas. Open your **eyes, ears and mind** to everything. The market place is changing constantly. What may be hot today could be cold and old news by tomorrow! Watch out for trends in the market place and think of how you can take advantage of them. Keep a very open mind here.

"Let the market decide what they want"

The biggest mistake you can make is to *assume* you know what the market wants and doesn't want. How do you know what's going on in consumers minds? You *don't*. And that is the point.

Let the market decide what they want; your job is to bring it to them.

> **"Assumption is one of the main reasons why so many eBay sellers and Internet marketers go broke!"**

Knowing and living by this one simple rule can make or break your eBay business. *Assumption* is one of the main reasons why so many eBay sellers and Internet marketers go broke!

From today forward, your 'two cents worth' as they say, no longer counts. If you conduct your market research properly you'll never have to assume what your market wants again because you'll know exactly what they want to buy.

And remember…your thoughts become your reality so if you think you won't find things to sell on eBay on an ongoing basis; you're right. But if you believe you can find a never-ending supply of stuff to sell, then it's guaranteed you will.

In the early stages of setting up a long-term eBay business you'll have to be active and you'll have to be patient. The deals will come to you once you get the word out that you're the master at selling on eBay. We've not met a single person who hasn't heard of eBay or one that doesn't have an 'eBay story' to tell.

During this journey…be open-minded and open hearted. You'll never think the same way again when it comes to business.

Look Around You. When you next walk into a department store, or any store for that matter, look around the place to see if you notice any 'new, hot items' that have come into the market place. **If they've made it to the shelves in department stores, they'll probably sell on eBay!**

You'll probably agree that just about every single week, a new product of some sort is introduced to the consumer market. It's a never-ending stream of products.

If you find something in a store you'd like to sell on eBay, look on the back of the packaging, and in most cases there'll be the manufactures details. **Get on the phone** and see if you can source the product. **Talk to people** in the store about doing a joint venture where you could sell their overstock or end of season clearance stuff.

When you get home, do your eBay research in completed listings and see if the products you see in stores are selling well on eBay. This is how we come up with so many ideas for products. They're all around us!

Use the Internet

You can go to 'Google' and type in 'trade show'. You'll see plenty of websites that will fill you in on where all the major trade shows are happening all around the world. There are over 4000 trade shows a year in America alone! Can you imagine whom you might meet at one of these expos? Matt and I have attended a massive trade show in China just recently. It was the biggest we've ever seen and it took us three full days just to get around all the stalls. The best thing about visiting a tradeshow is that you get to meet manufacturers and legitimate wholesalers. You can speak with them direct about selling products and you get to view the quality of the products, which is even more important.

To claim your **FREE** report and DVD (valued $97) go to
www.biddingbuzz.com/book

There are even online magazines available where you can access quality products from legitimate wholesalers. One that comes to mind is this website **www.asdamd.com** where you can find over 3500 suppliers who are happy to talk with you! Check it out for yourself and remember all this 'research' is tax deductible and necessary for long-term profits.

Walk around with your eyes and ears wide open. You'll begin to take notice of things you've never noticed before. It's called getting your 'eBay goggles' on. Matt and I find we constantly ask each other this question...

"Would that sell on eBay?"

Take Notes or Carry a Mini Hand Recorder. Write down or voice record everything you see that you may want to sell in your eBay business. **Carry a note pad or a mini recorder with you always...** You never know what ideas may pop into your head, anytime, anywhere! (We have a notepad with over 250 hot ideas we know will make money on eBay.)

The beauty about the notepad or mini recorder is that you may be out and about and during your conversations have people asking you whether 'this or that' would sell well on eBay. You can simply write the items down or record them and when you get home do your research. You might strike up a conversation and before you know it…you have a lead and you will want to write it down! We're constantly amazed at 'who knows who' and how many people are willing to help us get products once we get the word out.

> ## "We're constantly amazed at 'who knows who' and how many people are willing to help us get products once we get the word out"

This is a perfect way for you to develop relationships where you may end up selling other people's stuff for them, because they can't or don't want to know how to themselves.

You can use the notepad or recorder as a way to describe certain products or simply to get your ideas down as well as contact names and phone numbers.

There's nothing worse than being somewhere when someone is 'asking all the right questions' and you don't have your business card, or a pen and paper and we guarantee you'll have forgotten most of it within 24 hours!

Plan ahead…it could make you a fortune!

> *Sell what people want to buy…*
> *…not what you want to sell them!*

Step 3: Find and Research Hot, Untapped Markets, Start Selling and Watch the Profits Roll In.

"If you do just a little research, it is going to become evident to you that anyone that ever accomplished anything, did not know how they were going to do it. They only knew they were going to do it." **Bob Proctor**

"To be successful on eBay you need to get into the minds of your customers"

To be successful on eBay you need to get into the minds of your customers. What new products are people talking about? Can you sell them on eBay? To really get an edge, you need good market research. There are areas on the eBay website as well as many research tools to help you find the hot markets. Using eBay's completed listings area will let you know what your product or service is already selling for, so you know if you'll make money before you even get started.

eBay even have a 'hot list' of the most popular products for you to get ideas from. There's an area on the eBay homepage called 'eBay Pulse'.

This is where all the action is and where you can discover what people are searching for, the most popular products, the most watched items, the biggest stores as well as all the categories that are available for you to sell into.

Research is a critical part of your eBay business for long-term success. Have an abundance mindset – not a 'lack of' mindset. There is an abundance of items suitable for sale on eBay – do your research and find them.

Ongoing research is about building the foundations of your business just as if you were building your home – it is serious stuff. Use all your powers of observation while researching for new products – you never know when or where you might come across the next opportunity. Your local newsagent has a huge range of inexpensive specialist magazines you can use to research product ideas. Don't forget…if there's a magazine about it…someone is spending money on it.

Trade shows, industry magazines and even junk mail are another excellent source for researching new products. Never second-guess what the market wants to buy.

> **"Have an abundance mindset – not a 'lack of' mindset. There is an abundance of items suitable for sale on eBay – do your research and find them."**

Ultimately, your research should produce a product you have a back end for ongoing income. The term 'back end sale' applies to making an initial sale to a customer

> **"Research is constant, continuous, fun and extremely rewarding when you find a gold nugget!"**

To claim your **FREE** report and DVD (valued $97) go to
www.biddingbuzz.com/book

and then developing an ongoing sales relationship. Instead of just one sale and losing contact with the customer, by capturing the details of new customers, an opportunity exists for further sales in the future.

Research is constant, continuous, fun and extremely rewarding when you find a gold nugget! Again, we've made this simple for you... we show you exactly, step-by-step, live on video, how we find hot untapped markets on eBay using very simple software programs and recourses or you can do it yourself. We never sit there wracking our brains for ideas! Who's got time for that?

Step 4 : Choose Which Selling Format You Want To Use To Sell Your Items So You Can Maximise Your Profits Quickly & Easily.

To maximise your sales on eBay, we recommend you try different selling formats depending on what you're selling. Don't forget that people like to shop and buy in different ways. Also, it may come down to 'urgency' on the day or even one's 'mood'. The most popular choice for buying stuff on eBay is definitely the auction format, probably because of the 'thrill' people feel when trying to win an item - yes, it's addictive too, I might add ;-). However, the 'Buy It Now' option is best for those who want the item right now and can't wait for an auction to finish if there are still a few days to go.

It all comes down to experimenting and trying a variety of ways that will bring you the most profits.

A picture tells a thousand words...

OK, before you list your product for sale, it's super important that you have taken some great photos of it, so that buyers can see exactly what they're getting from you.

I really need to write a whole chapter about taking photos but there is a lot of information about this on the eBay website.

Here's a couple of hot tips for you though...

- Take clear, close up shots of your product with a plain background so buyers can clearly see what you're selling. A plain black or white background is good. Never have clutter in the background or you'll lose them!

If there are any flaws to your product, take a close up picture and honestly point it out. You will come across far more credible as a seller and people will feel better about trusting you.

- Have enough pictures of your item to make sure the bidder can clearly see what's on offer. At least show it at all angles so the buyer can get a good look at what you're selling.

- Photograph your item at close range with plenty of natural light.

- Give a detailed description so that your prospect becomes compelled to place a bid or buy from you.

- Don't forget to include things like brand name, size, color, defects, model, and anything else you think the buyer may need to know.

To claim your **FREE** report and DVD (valued $97) go to
www.biddingbuzz.com/book

Learning how to write great listing copy (the actual product description you include in your listing) is one of the main reasons why we, and so many of our members, make so much money on eBay.

There is massive power in the choice of words we use and again, we go into great detail about this at our live workshops and eBay Magic course. Master the art of writing great copy and you can write your own cheque. It is that powerful. You can find out more if you want by visiting,
www.biddingbuzz.com/book.html

OK, now let's explore the listing options a little further…

Auction Format

When you decide to choose the Auction format, you'll need to set a minimum starting bid. This is mandatory and can be as low as 1 cent or as high as you choose, but keep in mind that **if you start your bidding too high, potential bidders will be turned off** because they want to feel like they may be able to snap up a bargain.

By starting your bidding low, you'll definitely encourage bidders to bid on your auction and with a bit of luck, your auction may even start a bidding frenzy. People seem to take more interest in auctions that already have bids on them because they feel that there is more demand for your item and will feel it's worth owning themselves.

With the auction format, you can decide on the auction duration, which could be a 1 day, 3 day, 5 day, 7 day or 10 day auction.

From our experience though we usually only list each item as a single item so that the bidders don't know exactly how many items you have available. If they feel that you have lots of the same item then they may just decide to come back another time. As we all know though, life goes on and if they don't take action immediately you could lose them to another sellers item.

You can see in the next example that you can also choose to donate a percentage of your sale to charity and, finally, you have the option to schedule your listing too.

This is a point you might want to think about. Of course you want to be finishing your auction when most people are online looking for your type of item.

And don't be fooled into thinking that every listing on eBay gets the best price on a Sunday night between 6-8pm even though plenty of 'experts' spruik this.

> **"Don't be fooled into thinking that every listing on eBay gets the best price on a Sunday night between 6-8pm even though plenty of 'experts' spruik this"**

You must know your own market and know how to use the research tools available to your advantage.

Don't guess…it'll cost you too much money!

We can't express enough, just how important this part of the process is. Don't turn this business into a guessing game…there's enough

To claim your **FREE** report and DVD (valued $97) go to
www.biddingbuzz.com/book

data out there for you to be able to truly optimise every chance of making the most profits you can.

Remember…eBay is your business and it must make a profit to make it worth your while.

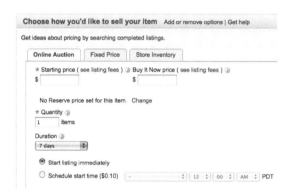

Setting A Reserve Price For Your Auction

Depending on the country you're in, you might have the option to set a **Reserve Price** for your auction. The Reserve is different from the Start Price because the bidders don't actually get to see what the reserve amount is.

So what can happen is that buyers can place their bid and if it's not higher than the reserve, then the bidder is told that the reserve is not met. **This forces the bidder to place another bid**. This can have the affect of annoying the bidder if they have to keep placing bids and still not have a live auction.

You would consider using the reserve option to protect yourself if you have a **high-ticket** item and don't want to risk letting it go too cheap. **This can be a good thing** if you still want to let people play the game, rather than setting a high start price that might put off potential bidders.

Using the Auction Format & the 'Buy It Now' Format in the Same Listing

Starting bid:	**US $27.00**	
Your maximum bid:	**US $** [ ]	**Place Bid >**
	(Enter US $27.00 or more)	
Buy It Now price:	**US $29.00**	**Buy It Now >**
	Immediate payment required	

It's also possible to have a **Starting Bid** and a **'Buy It Now'** option in the same auction. If this is the case, and someone places a bid at the Start Price, then the **Buy It Now** option disappears.

Dutch Auctions

If you're selling large quantities of en exact same item, another way for you to sell your items could be by using the **Multiple Item or Dutch Auction** method. Just like traditional auctions, Dutch auctions can run for 1,3,5,7 or 10 days.

Put simply, if you were selling identical bracelets and had 100 to sell, you could list the whole lot in the one listing. **Bidders would then bid on the quantity they would like, and the amount they were prepared to pay for each bracelet.**

The price of each bracelet is determined by the price offered by **each bidder**. All winning bidders then pay the amount they bid for the item and can then purchase as many of the items as they choose.

To claim your **FREE** report and DVD (valued $97) go to
www.biddingbuzz.com/book

There is a formula used to determine who the winning bidders are, and the amount of items they can buy. The bidders who offer the highest amount per item, get to choose how many items they want, then the next highest bidder can choose how many they want and so on until all the items are sold.

If you were to sell using this format, you always put in a start price and in many cases this can become the lowest bid amount.

If you're lucky enough to have a 'bidding war' occur with your bidders, rebids must be higher than the total of that particular bidder's past bids.

There are a few rules when it comes to doing this type of listing. Firstly you must be eBay verified.

You must have a feedback rating of 30 or higher OR you must have been registered on eBay for 14 days or more, OR if you have a PayPal account and you accept PayPal as a payment method your feedback rating will only then need to be 15.

To calculate your fees here's how it works. Your listing fee is a calculation of your opening bid multiplied by the number of items in your auction. However, the maximum listing fee can vary depending on what listing upgrades you might choose to use.

Your final value fees are based on your total in dollars sold.
Just finishing up here, it's important to know that as a 'buyer' when bidding on a Dutch auction, you can't proxy bid. Proxy bidding is when you simply enter your highest bid that you're willing to pay for an item and eBay bids on your behalf.

Finally, winning bidders have the right to refuse partial quantities of items you're selling, if they miss out on the quantity that they wanted in the first place.

I know Dutch auctions can sound a little confusing, and if you'd like to learn more about them, you can use eBay's help area.

Fixed Price Format

The **Fixed Price format** or the **'Buy It Now'** as it's commonly known, allows you to sell items for the price you want, and not have to worry that you might lose money in an auction. These listings still appear in the standard auction search results, and have a listing duration option, just like a standard auction, of 1,3,5,7 or 10 days.

In addition if you have a eBay Store you will also get the bonus advantage of being able to list for 30 days or Good Till Cancelled, which means indefinitely till you cancel the listing.

Also having a quantity in your listing can help you with your sales history in Best Match and now with new eBay changes you can only list 1 Fixed Price listing for the one item so it is key to use a quantity to rate higher in the search results.

There are many reasons why you'd choose to sell items in this way, and in fact, you could have **Fixed Price** listings along with **Auction** style listings and see which gives you a better result.

Ultimately, by conducting your market research you'll know which format works best for the items you're selling, and at what price point your buyers are prepared to pay for it.

What is good about the Fixed Price option is that your listings appear in the search results. This means you have access to the multitudes of traffic eBay has and have a much better chance of selling your items.

Classified Ads Format

You can now use **Classified Ads** to list things like **services, properties, and individual items** that you want to generate multiple leads for. The difference with this format is that buyers and sellers are not able to transact online though eBay. Also with Classified Ads, there is no Feedback given or received by either party.

The main features of Classified Ads are...

- You list your asking price, and any negotiations happens offline between the two interested parties. There is no bidding available.

- Interested buyers who see your ad actually fill out a contact form where their information is then sent to you.

- Or, you can include your contact details in the listing and allow people to contact you direct (fantastic way to generate leads).

- You can list your service or property for a specific period of time, 30 days, 60 days, 90 days.

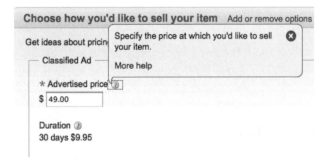

As you can see there are many options available to you when it comes to selling your items on eBay. As with anything new, we recommend that you test and measure the results you get from each of the different types of selling strategies.

We recommend you look at this as a long-term project and test your results, measuring things like...

- The auction duration

- The selling format

- The time you start and finish your auctions

To claim your **FREE** report and DVD (valued $97) go to
www.biddingbuzz.com/book

- The amount of listings you have live and which days to sell

- The pictures you include in the listings

- The written description or copy writing you include in the listing

- And much more.

Remember this is a mixture of experience, skill and product research. Many people make the mistake of trying to take a particular product to the market place, before they know if there is actually a market for it and people are prepared to spend money buying it from you.

> **"Many people make the mistake of trying to take a particular product to the market place, before they know if there is actually a market for it and people are prepared to spend money buying it from you"**

Also we always like to think long term too, rather than just hit and miss or a fad business. After all, it's about creating a sustainable lifestyle from your online business and, even if takes longer initially to find the niche market you want to get into, it's definitely better in the long run.

Step 5: How To Give Your Customers Outstanding Service So They'll Become Raving Fans, Shop With You Over And Over Again And Help You Grow Your Profits Beyond Your Wildest Dreams!

This is by far the most important area too many eBay sellers ignore! What are they thinking? Without happy customers there is no business. You'll want to create 'evangelists' so that your business automatically grows via word of mouth. You have no idea just how powerful this can be till you experience it.

> **"Without happy customers there is no business"**

Remember, eBay shoppers can't see you or get a feel for what type of person you are to the degree they could if they were to chat with you personally.

You don't have a retail shop front so it's normal that new customers may have some reservations about handing over money – this is why customer service is paramount on eBay.

Our whole business is built on referrals because we provide outstanding customer service. We have found that around 95% of eBay sellers assume the transaction is complete when the sale has been made and they have banked the money – in fact, we believe this is just the beginning. If you are friendly and kind to your customers they will refer other customers to you – this is word-of-mouth advertising, the least expensive and best advertising of all for attracting people to your business.

To claim your **FREE** report and DVD (valued $97) go to
www.biddingbuzz.com/book

> ## "95% of eBay sellers assume the transaction is complete when the sale has been made and they have banked the money – in fact, we believe this is just the beginning"

Think about the last time you had a get-together with your family or friends in your home. You vacuumed, mopped and even dusted the top shelves; you stored the kids' toys where they belong, double-checked that your bathrooms were spotless, and tidied up a little more than usual.

When your guests arrived, you were the gracious host; you were wearing your million-dollar smile, offering drinks, serving food, plenty of laughs and stories. They in turn, were the grateful guests, enjoying the attention, basking in your warm welcome, feasting on food and drinks and promising to reciprocate very soon, as it was just so much fun!

Now, think about the most recent shoppers and potential customers who visited your eBay store, or who will be if you're just getting started.
"How were they, or will they be treated?"

Did you, and will you, offer them a similar taste of the gracious service and hospitality you displayed for your friends or family?

> ## "Everyone talks it up when it comes to customer service, but it takes more than words to excel at it"

If you have to stop and think about it, you probably didn't or wouldn't have.

Everyone talks it up when it comes to customer service, but it takes more than words to excel at it. You must learn how to go beyond good customer service, and achieve outstanding customer service, so that your customers become evangelists for your business.

Only when you achieve this will you have something to talk about—and so will your customers.

Achieving great customer service has a lot to do with understanding customer expectations. And the bottom line is that excelling at customer service can expand your bottom line…big time.

Before we go on though, **let's just clarify for you the different types of customers you'll come across,** and how each type of customer can play a massive role in the growth of your business…or not.

The Suspect

People, who haven't heard about your product or service, yet may want it some time in the future. Or maybe someone who is still info shopping and needs more information before they even qualify themselves as a prospect.

To claim your **FREE** report and DVD (valued $97) go to
www.biddingbuzz.com/book

A good example might be someone who has all of a sudden decided to go on a diet because summer is looming. They're now looking for products or services that will help them achieve their desired outcomes, yet a few days ago, the thought had never entered their mind.

The Prospect

People who are interested in your product or service, have heard about you, but haven't yet made the decision to actually buy from you. They'll be looking for more information to determine what you or your product is like before they can make a buying decision.

The Customer

These are people who know about you and your product or service. They're happy to buy from you here and there, as they know they'll get what they ordered, but they're not necessarily committed to you in any way. They'll more than likely shop around for the best deals. This happens a lot when it comes to eBay, however, you can create those 'evangelists' if you really put your mind to it. It is a fact that people do not just buy on price alone, but they do buy based on the 'experience'.

The Client

This is a customer who buys from you on a regular basis. They like and trust you and are happy to keep buying from you, because they know what to expect. They don't necessarily talk about you but will usually stay loyal.

The Advocate

This is a customer who recommends you and your business, if asked about your product or service. They can even be a second hand referrer, and not have used your services or bought from you at this stage. They may have heard through the 'grapevine' how good your products and services are, so naturally feel compelled to drop your name if asked.

The Evangelist

A customer who recommends you, and your business, to everyone they know; even if your product or service hasn't been brought up or asked about in the conversation! This is the exact type of customer that will help grow your business faster. They will buy anything and everything from you in a lot of cases.

They simply can't get enough of what you have to offer and will refer all their closet friends and even strangers to you. **These customers are pure gold and your business' biggest asset! Treat them with respect and look after them as you would your own family.**

From the explanations above, **you can now see why you'd want as many of your customers to become evangelists for your business as you can!**

We're now going to explore some more simple, easy ways that you can implement into your business, immediately, that will ensure your success at building amazing customer relations.

To claim your **FREE** report and DVD (valued $97) go to
www.biddingbuzz.com/book

Step 6 : Why Keeping and Maintaining A 100% Positive Feedback Score Is Your Number One Priority In Your eBay Business.

As you'll agree, running an eBay business is quite different to running a 'bricks and mortar' type of business. One of the main differences is that with an online business, your buyers or customers can't see you, so they don't know exactly whom they may be buying from.

In a 'bricks and mortar' business, the owner has a chance to create and nurture great customer relations by providing outstanding service, a good range of products, return policies, friendly staff etc.

When you experience these 'good shopping experiences', you tend to go back and shop with these people, over and over again... because you know without a doubt that you will enjoy the shopping experience. Every time.

Sometimes price and location does not come into it, if the experience is extremely positive.

"People love to shop where they'll feel welcome and appreciated. It's a fact!"

The one thing shoppers can see by looking at your eBay business though, is your '**Detailed Seller Rating**'. This feedback rating has basic information about past transactions that you have completed, and what the overall experience was like for the people you dealt with.

Every eBay member has a feedback rating. For serious eBay sellers, this rating is 'jealously guarded' because your feedback rating is all you have when it comes to building your credibility in this business. Every comment about the way you conduct business, good or bad, counts.

The feedback shown below is a snap shot of our feedback around March 2009. It has the total amount of unique feedback left as well as a number of other icons. People on eBay love seeing the icons after your Seller ID, so get as many as you can.

We have at the time of printing 2997 Feedback with the…

Red Star
Power Seller icon
About Me page icon
eBay Store icon
eBay Guides icon
Top Reviewer icon

All of these icons build credibility with the buyer and also confidence in their minds that we are a trusted and credible seller on eBay.

At a glance, your potential customers or buyers can see what other buyers and sellers have to say about you. They'll see how well, or how poorly you've conducted business in the past, and how trustworthy you are as a seller.

To claim your **FREE** report and DVD (valued $97) go to
www.biddingbuzz.com/book

On the next page is a sample of what a feedback rating looks like on a member's eBay page. This is another account we have, to showcase to our members the different strategies we use. It's not our main selling account but rather another live training tool we have.

The number of feedback ratings is the number in the brackets. Both the **buyer** and the **seller** are the only ones who may leave feedback for each other.

Sometimes you'll notice a little coloured star beside the number of feedbacks in the brackets. There are 10 different coloured stars for you to earn, and each colour automatically appears as you grow your feedback score.

Here's how the 'Stars' work.

When you first open your eBay account, you have zero feedback and therefore no star. When you achieve your first 10 feedback ratings, you automatically get a Yellow Star beside your feedback rating.

You get a **Blue Star** when you receive a feedback of 50 to 99 feedback points.

You get a **Turquoise Star** when you achieve 100 to 499 feedback points.

You get a **Purple Star** when you achieve 500 to 999 feedback points.

You get a **Red Star** when you achieve 1,000 to 4,999 feedback points.

You get a **Green Star** when you achieve 5,000 to 9,999 feedback points.

You get a **Yellow Shooting Star** when you achieve 10,000 to 24,999 feedback points.

You get a **Turquoise Shooting Star** when you achieve 25,000 to 49,999 feedback points.

You get a **Purple Shooting Star** when you achieve 50,000 to 99,999 feedback points.

You get a **Red Shooting Star** when you achieve 100,000 or higher.

If you're a buyer, and considering bidding or purchasing something from any eBay seller, it's always a good idea to click the feedback rating/score and read through some of the comments that have been left by other members.

While a **high feedback** score is a good sign, still read through the comments to see if there's any negative feedback that will effect your buying decision.

To claim your **FREE** report and DVD (valued $97) go to
www.biddingbuzz.com/book

Below is exactly what will appear on your screen when you click on the feedback score within the brackets of a Seller ID.

So, Exactly How Does The Feedback System Work?

The eBay feedback system is quite simple. Here's how it works.

POSITIVE

You get **+1 point** added to your feedback score for **each positive** comment and rating left for you.

NEUTRAL

You get **0 points** added to your feedback score for **each neutral** comments and rating left for you.

NEGATIVE

You get **-1 point** to your feedback score for each **negative comment** and rating left for you.

You get your first **feedback star** when you reach a feedback score of **10** or **more** comments and ratings left for you.

In the example on the previous page, there are 157 feedbacks. Underneath the member profile area, you can read all the feedback left for this member, good, bad, or otherwise.

The feedback percentage is now calculated over a 12-month period instead of the original total that the system previously used.

This change was made to ensure that the most recent feedback being left actually reflected the current service being provided. There were cases where the feedback levels were so high from years of selling, that even recent negative feedback wasn't affecting the percentages.

Here's How To Gain Credibility In Your Chosen Market So You'll Stand Head And Shoulders Above Your Competitors!
It's a well-known fact that people in general are skeptical. This is especially true when people are shopping on the Internet.

This is totally understandable, as there have been many Internet sellers who have done the wrong thing, and as a result, many shoppers are now wary.

Thankfully, eBay boasts an online reputation of having a 99.99% secure transaction record, giving the eBay market place amazing credibility.

To claim your **FREE** report and DVD (valued $97) go to
www.biddingbuzz.com/book

> **"Thankfully, eBay boasts an online reputation of having a 99.99% secure transaction record, giving the eBay market place amazing credibility."**

You too need to build a solid foundation of credibility and believability with your eBay business. Potential customers need to know that you're qualified to be giving them advice on how you can solve their problem. Your feedback rating will help overcome this potential problem.

This is all part of building trust with your reader. And there's no better way to build trust with someone, than if you come across credible, knowledgeable, trustworthy, and genuine. Remember, people aren't stupid; they can usually detect B.S. when they see it.

Another way to gain trust with your potential bidders is having a fantastic feedback rating where they can see at a glance how other shoppers enjoyed their shopping experience with you. It's normal in this business for shoppers to be wary of you, if you have an extremely low feedback rating.

> **"And there's no better way to build trust with someone, than if you come across credible, knowledgeable, trustworthy, and genuine"**

For example, top marketers include customer testimonials in much of their marketing and advertising. It's been proven time and time again to be a very effective tool to make the new potential customer feel comfortable buying from you. You'll even notice we do it in this book.

It's the same on eBay!

"People want to know that other people have bought your product first, and that they've lived to tell the tale."

Not only that, they're willing to write about it, and tell you how good the experience was, and how by owning the product, their life has improved for the better. That's why your feedback rating is so critical to your eBay business. The more positive feedbacks you have, the more comfortable people will feel, bidding for your items.

And the best part is, with a higher feedback rating, you'll get more bids, higher final values for your items, and your business will ultimately expand beyond your wildest dreams!

A good listing description builds credibility with the reader as they see that you know what you're talking about. It helps to establish yourself as an expert in your chosen field, and everybody feels more comfortable buying from a seller who knows his or her stuff.

After all, wouldn't you want to deal with a person like this?

To finish up here, you can see why eBay sellers are so protective of their 'feedback' rating and will go to great measures to make sure they give the best service they can. If you concentrate on this part, the rest will fall into place for you. Don't be scared of negative feedback by the way…it happens to the best of us and I can still recall the first time we got a negative. I nearly started crying and even rang the customer to see why he'd given a negative to me. He didn't really understand how important it was and said he didn't really have a complaint.

To claim your **FREE** report and DVD (valued $97) go to
www.biddingbuzz.com/book

Thankfully he did remove it but, since then, of course we've gone on to get a few more as we sold larger volumes of items.

The great thing that can come from negative feedback is that you will automatically 'lift your game' and do everything possible so that it doesn't happen again. In hindsight, it's can be a very positive thing that will help you become a better business person, even though at the time it won't feel this way.

Step 7: Automate Your eBay Business up to 90% and You Will Experience 'Freedom' like You Never Have Before... Guaranteed.

This is by far the most exciting aspect of having an eBay business and one that we are very passionate about. We love talking about the automation process because it's only through automation that you can truly be free of the day-to-day tasks of running an eBay business. Once you experience what this is like, you will never go back, as they say ;-)

Because we automated nearly 90% of our own eBay business within months of starting it, we were free to be able to create our eBay Magic home study course which hundreds of people are now using all over the world. The most exciting part of this is not only do we still have our highly profitable eBay business running in less than 10 hours a week, we have finally stepped up to where we both truly belong... and that's mentoring, sharing and helping others achieve the same. We could not be happier in fact.

> ## "It's only through automation that you can truly be free of the day-to-day tasks of running an eBay business"

> ### "We automated nearly 90% of our own eBay business within months of starting it"

In truth, the automation process is one of the main reasons why people find eBay such an attractive business to be involved with. We've had many businesses in the past and have never been able to automate the process like we can with eBay.

The automation process allows you to either sit back and enjoy the fruits of your labour, or move into another untapped market and go again! Truly amazing, isn't it?

So what are some of the things you can automate in your eBay business to free up the majority of your day?

> ## "In truth, the automation process is one of the main reasons why people find eBay such an attractive business to be involved with"

Below are the daily processes we have automated, which frees up our time to the point where our business now takes less than 10 hours a week to run, and so can you. Beautiful.

- **The listing process**. That's putting items up for auction or the 'buy it now' format. If you can sell the same items (or cluster of items) over and over again, this is a very simple process to automate. As soon as you sell an item the system automatically relists it according to your automated instructions.

- **Our customer payment reminder emails.** Once the sale has been made we can set the automation rules up to gently remind the customer of payment within a certain time frame. The beauty of this is that you're never chasing people for payment. The system does it for you and it works beautifully.

- **eBay feedback.** You can automate this process so that immediately when someone buys from you, the system will leave them positive feedback right away. The great thing about this is that your customer will be prompted to do the same for you and it leaves a great feeling of buyer satisfaction.

- **Invoicing and checkout.** As soon as someone buys an item from you, the system automatically sends them an eBay invoice and lets them know how to make a payment. No waiting, no chasing, no pain. Too easy.

- **Payments and banking.** As soon as your customer has made a payment, the system lets you know, so that you can ship right away. If the customer pays via PayPal (which eBay owns) you will see a little $ sign beside the product they bought in your my eBay area, indicating payment has been successfully made. It's so easy and user friendly.

- **'Item sent' emails.** As soon as you ship the item to your customer they will automatically receive your email letting them know their parcel is on the way! They're happy, you're happy and it all happens in a split second!

- **Data collection.** This is your 'book work' part. The bit that most of us hate! eBay have it all sorted out for you so that each month you can see exactly what's happening in your business financially.

How much money you've made, how much the cost of your items were, how much your eBay fees are, how much your postage costs and charges were and finally how much profit you made.

This information is the most important information to collect of all because too many eBay sellers think they are making big money when in fact they're going broke. They simply don't know how to keep financial records and it really is so easy. You can see at a glance how you're going for the month and plan for the future like big companies do and you should!

- **Second chance offers and much more!** Here's where you can really get the edge on your competitors because they have no idea how to make the most of this offer. A 'second chance offer' means that if you're selling an item that you have more than one of, you have the chance to sell it to the losing bidder if their bid was close enough to the winning bid. In fact, depending on how many of these same items you have, you can offer the product to as many 'losing bidders' as you like depending on the price you're happy to settle for.

This is an awesome tool and we sell so many items this way. Can you imagine how much more profit we make just sending out second chance offers? A lot. Not only that, you don't have to pay the 'insertion

To claim your **FREE** report and DVD (valued $97) go to
www.biddingbuzz.com/book

fee' when someone takes you up on your second chance offer. Perfect if you sell a regular cluster of products!

Can you see the absolute power in this type of business now? I can't type fast enough I have so much to share with you!

> **"Can you see the absolute power in this type of business now?"**

For many people an automated eBay business is a serious – and fun – alternative to working long hours of paid, or worse, unpaid overtime to supplement their income. You can now see why we are so passionate about the possibilities eBay can bring you.

> **"For many people an automated eBay business is a serious – and fun – alternative to working long hours of paid, or worse, unpaid overtime to supplement their income"**

Chapter 16

hy Having A Mentor
Will Save Your Time And Money

Chapter 16 : Why Getting A Mentor...

"You can always get more money but never more time"

What can we say? We feel that we have both gone over this point and the importance of it many times throughout this book. I think by now you understand and can see why we so strongly recommend you doing the same.

I have a saying I learnt from one of my favourite mentors, Mal Emery, and it goes like this... "You can always get more money but never more time."

And he also says, "Pay once, cry once." (Meaning the investment into business education as opposed to spending the time trying to figure it out the hard way yourself).

We love this because as he says, you're going to pay one way or another for your education. That's in time or money. The question we have for you is...

Which is less painful for you right now?

These words are always foremost in our mind when we're looking at any business opportunity and every time we discuss business, we're always asking ourselves how we can fast track the processes by following a proven system someone else has already created.

> **"You're going to pay one way or another for your education. That's in time or money"**

I don't know about you, but we are well over wasting precious time stuffing around trying to work things out for ourselves when we can simply invest in our education and avoid the heartache of costly, embarrassing mistakes. We know we can always replace the money (investment) but never the time wasted let alone the headspace it's cost you!

> **"We are well over wasting precious time stuffing around trying to work things out for ourselves when we can simply invest in our education and avoid the heartache of costly, embarrassing mistakes"**

Here's us speaking in the UK to over 4,000 people. Our biggest crowd yet and boy were we nervous! But we managed to get through it while still having fun.

Ask yourself the same question; do you really have time to waste trying to work all this out for yourself?

We believe we know the answer if you truly value your time.

So now that you know a whole lot more about how to make money on eBay (and we haven't even scratched the surface yet) are you excited about setting up an eBay business and creating the exact lifestyle that you want and deserve too?

Right now, write down all the things that you'd like to be spending the extra money on and how you'd like your day to pan out each day, if you had your own way. The more detail you include the more detail the universe has to be able to deliver it to you.

Go on, start to imagine and visualize exactly how your own highly profitable eBay business is going to look and feel like, once you get cracking on it.

> **"Right now, write down all the things that you'd like to be spending the extra money on and how you'd like your day to pan out each day, if you had your own way"**

To claim your **FREE** report and DVD (valued $97) go to
www.biddingbuzz.com/book

"... if you want success in any field, you must learn from mentors who already have the results you're looking for and model them exactly"

Matt and Amanda Clarkson

Chapter 17

ow To Ensure Ongoing Success
With Your eBay Business

Becoming a successful eBay Seller is all about doing the opposite to what the bulk of the other sellers are doing. In most cases people have learned by trial and error when it comes to selling on eBay. This means that quite often they are just making the same mistakes that the other uneducated sellers are making and not really maximizing the full potential of eBay.

> **"Becoming a successful eBay Seller is all about doing the opposite to what the bulk of the other sellers are doing"**

Here's a list of what not to do, followed up by some great tips on how to ensure that you're on the right track to creating a super successful eBay business...

Did you know that around 54% of everything listed for sale on eBay never even gets a bid - let alone sells?

Here's why:

- 95% of sellers on eBay don't have a clue what they're really doing

- Items are listed in the wrong categories and as a result buyers never find the listing

- Some sellers buy large amounts of stock and can't resell it

- They don't know how to research and find a profitable niche market

To claim your **FREE** report and DVD (valued $97) go to
www.biddingbuzz.com/book

- They don't know what their competitors are up to

- They have no idea how to source items to sell at high profits

- They don't know how to write compelling listings that get bidders to take action

- They have too much negative feedback from customers

- They don't know how to ship items properly or make money doing it

- They are not experts in their chosen category and waste thousands of dollars on eBay fees every month

- They have no idea how to give great customer service

- They don't know a cold market from a hot market

- They get suspended from eBay for listing violations

- They don't know how to create multiple streams of income through their eBay business

- They finish auctions at the wrong time of the day - this can cost you big time!

- They lose money on incorrect shipping costs and policies

- They get too many returned items which brings negative feedback

- They have no idea on how to automate any part of the daily tasks, which is the most important aspect as it gives you the freedom you truly desire!

And the list goes on!

Imagine how much time and effort it would take for you to try to go it alone and work all this out the hard way? We haven't even scratched the surface of what we'd love to show you about making money on eBay. Not even close to it in fact!

Don't worry because you can easily avoid all of these costly pitfalls because we've already been down this road and succeeded beyond everyone's wildest expectations.

It's now our passion and mission to share our wealth of knowledge with those who desire the type of life we now live because of our eBay business. Unfortunately, most people only dream about the kind of life we lead, but in truth, anyone can have it if they put their mind to it.

Here are some helpful tips so that you can avoid these costly mistakes and make profits instead of loses.

- Be very careful and only source those products you KNOW buyers want to buy, and NOT what you want to sell them!

- Study your market place and never assume anything. You don't know what people are thinking or feeling about certain products.

- Be ready to roll up your sleeves and work hard in the early stages of your eBay business. This is called 'setting your foundation for long-term success'. It's not hard and you'll enjoy the process.

To claim your **FREE** report and DVD (valued $97) go to
www.biddingbuzz.com/book

- Don't keep all of your profits. Re-invest back into growing your online presence. You'd be amazed at how quickly you can grow your product base, which brings even more profits.

- Find legitimate wholesalers and manufacturers and distributors. They are out there - you just have to look hard! We've given you enough ideas and links to last you a lifetime!

- Margins on eBay are small. This is a fact of life in the eBay world, so buy smart. This game is like real estate…. you make your money going in! There are hundreds of un-tapped categories on eBay just waiting for you to take advantage of that will make you a very nice income.

- Be careful when you are first starting out that you don't lose money with all the eBay and PayPal fees incurred. This is a common mistake amongst a lot of eBay sellers in the early days.

You think you're making great profits until you get your monthly statement from eBay, only to find that most of your hard earned profits got sucked up in fees. Do your sums properly taking into account all the costs and you won't get caught here.

- **Use caution** when buying in bulk. You know why!

- When you feel overwhelmed at times, **remember these five points**. Keep an open mind, Keep your eyes peeled, Take notes or record your ideas and thoughts, Research, Source.

- Education is the key. Attend seminars to develop your mindset, and if you can, attend the next eBay Live seminar held once a year. We guarantee it'll change how you see and run your eBay business forever. Not only that, it's so much fun you'll be sad to see it end!

"Education is the key. Attend seminars to develop your mindset"

- **Be disciplined**. Like all elite athletes, to be the best in your chosen field, you must choose discipline and take action. Without these two ingredients you can forget it!

- **Be time managed**. Get all the important things like marketing, product re-sourcing, research and listings out of the way during the time of the day when you feel most energized. Then, do all the other bits and pieces like wrapping packages and going to the post office etc later in the day. You'll find that you get so much more out of your day!

- Remember, better product sourcing, leads to higher $$$$$ sales for you!

- Don't worry if you feel overwhelmed at times. We all do. Just take a break, have a cuppa and something to eat and you'll feel refreshed and ready to go again. Remember…this is not a race. You're going at your own pace. Enjoy the process.

- Have fun and enjoy this business. Selling on eBay can be a very rewarding business once you're up and running. It's fun, entertaining, interactive and challenging. There are not too many businesses in the world like this, so nurture what you have and enjoy the lifestyle it can bring you.

You know, starting and maintaining a very successful eBay business is very achievable for just about anyone willing to do the work that is

To claim your **FREE** report and DVD (valued $97) go to
www.biddingbuzz.com/book

necessary to make it happen. You just have to decide that you're going to 'go for it' and make a start.

> **"Don't worry if you feel overwhelmed at times. We all do. Just take a break, have a cuppa and something to eat and you'll feel refreshed and ready to go again"**

When we first started selling on eBay, we didn't have a clue what we were doing. We'd never bought one thing off eBay, yet alone understood how it all worked! The first thing we did was open a 'buyers' account and got to know what it would be like to be the customer.

> **"It's fun, entertaining, interactive and challenging. There are not too many businesses in the world like this, so nurture what you have and enjoy the lifestyle it can bring you"**

The things we looked out for were: customer service, payment methods, shipping times, packaging quality, the condition of the product and how the overall experience was.

This is a perfect way for you to 'break the ice' if you haven't already done so. As a Seller on eBay, you must step into the shoes of your customers and run your whole business based on the customers 'buying experience' within your business. Imagine…if you were to buy something from yourself, what would that buying experience be like?

The trick is, start off slow and steady, and build and grow as your confidence and knowledge expands. You may want to try a couple of different methods of acquiring stock before you make your final decision.

> **"The trick is, start off slow and steady, and build and grow as your confidence and knowledge expands."**

Unfortunately I have to stop here, which pains me let me tell you! We love sharing all the money making ways with you, and we still have at least five more we could share but can't today. You see, there are just so many juicy ways you can be up and running on eBay in no time at all. You've just got to know what you're doing and why you're doing it.

Once you've got the step-by-step system in front of you, there's no holding back. You can now see why you can create as many cash flow streams as you desire.

> **"Once you've got the step-by-step system in front of you, there's no holding back and you can now see why you can create as many cash flow streams as you desire."**

Remember... You are only limited by your own thoughts and beliefs.

7 Traits Of An eBay Seller Who Makes Consistent Income All Year Round...

1. They are 100% focused and know that mistakes made along the way will only bring them to success faster!

2. They put in the hard yards and understand that a real business is built on a solid foundation, which takes massive action and hard work in the beginning to create.

3. They understand that their outcome is an exact result of what they put into their business on a daily basis and never blame others.

4. They systemise their business as quickly as possible, so they can they work on it, not in it.

5. They work at becoming product-sourcing experts and understand the value of building relationships with suppliers.

6. They're big on giving outstanding customer service to keep their buyers coming back for more.

7. They treat their eBay like a real business, never a hobby.

Would you like some FREE Gifts & Some extra Handholding along the way?

Thank you for taking the time to read this book. If you got this far, it's probable you're serious about making something happen and you'd like to investigate this further, right? More than anyone, we understand exactly how you feel about venturing into the world of selling on eBay and know that once you start making automated cash flow day in, day out, and living life on your own terms, instead of someone elses', you will never go back.

Just like a rubber band that has been really stretched… …you'll never go back to normal.

You'll agree we've not even 'scratched the surface' here of what we'd like to show you, but hope that you've had your eyes and mind opened to endless possibilities, and smarter, better ways for you to make fast, easy money and more importantly, ways you can now free up your time so you can enjoy your days more with less worry.

Most importantly though, we hope you too feel that you've perhaps found answers you've been looking for, for so long…

However, the fact is that when it comes to truly creating a highly successful eBay business, it's going to take more than just the basics you have seen in this book. We've shown you some of the possibilities available to you and you've seen some of the steps you can take to help you become successful…

To claim your **FREE** report and DVD (valued $97) go to
www.biddingbuzz.com/book

But what if you had the whole treasure map laid out before you with every step shown? What if this treasure map showed you every pitfall and booby trap that you may encounter, but with the unknown and highly sought after "Cheat Sheet" that would take you safely around the obstacles you will come across, and lead you safely around them to the prize you're really looking for?

The lifestyle you've been searching for that will give you more choices, more options, more money and more time to spend your life the way you always dreamed of…

All you've got to do is take the first step and the rest is easy! We'll even hold your hand along the way if that's what you want. Never have there been so many closely guarded eBay secrets, strategies and tips all laid out on a silver platter for you to take massive advantage of. Right Now.

No matter what style of learning appeals to you, we've covered it in our eBay Magic programs. Our successful members include everyday people ranging from children as young as 5 (with mum and dad's help of course ;-) right through to mature people of 84 years young.

So what about you though? Do you want more from this life?

Now we have reached the end of the book, you might be wondering what the next step is? If you would like to find out more and see if eBay is going to be your wealth vehicle too, then here's what to do next.

As a special thank you for reading our book we've put together a **FREE DVD** and **REPORT** on how you can go from Zero To A Million & Beyond on eBay, **Valued at $97 PLUS A FREE** Downloadable Gift. An MP3 recording of Amanda talking about how to build a saleable eBay business and turn it into an asset **Valued at another $200 (Total FREE assets value $297)**…simply visit the website below, enter your details into our secure and fully private online form and **we will rush your Report and DVD out to you.**

www.biddingbuzz.com/book.html

To claim your **FREE** report and DVD (valued $97) go to
www.biddingbuzz.com/book

"In any moment a decision you make can change the course of your life forever...The very next person you stand behind in line or sit next to on an airplane, the very next phone call you make or receive. The very next movie you see or book you read or page you turn could be the one single thing that causes the floodgates to open, and all of the things that you've been waiting for to fall into place."

Anthony Robbins

"Many of us waste time on petty worries or frivolities, but those who know the value of how limited time is seem to cherish every moment they have as a gift. "

Shadonna Richards

To claim your **FREE** report and DVD (valued $97) go to
www.biddingbuzz.com/book

REE BONUS

Claim Your
REE Report, Your
/D & Special
dio MP3 Gift
th A Total Value
$297 visit...

w.biddingbuzz.com/book

Chapter 18

eBay Magic Success Stories...

Cathy & Alex make over $35,000 every month in their eBay Business

"We attended the eBay Magic workshop and invested in the Super Course, back in November 2007. After the seminar, we decided to take the plunge into investing in advanced mentoring with Matt, Amanda and the team. Since that time, we have both left our old jobs, become silver Power sellers ($6,000 per month) (with gold in our sights) and are in the process of importing products from overseas.

Matt, Amanda and all the other Bidding Buzz crew have all been there to help us every step of the way. Our business is about 90% automated now, allowing us to have more free time than we ever thought possible. By the end of September this year, we're now turning over $35,000 per month. It's sounds a bit corny, but looking back at what our lives were like less than a year ago, the future is now a lot brighter. We're looking forward to expanding into other areas soon, and increasing our profits even more. We truly believe that if we had started this adventure on our own, we would not be anywhere close to where we are now – in such a short period of time."

Kathy & Alex Romano, Gold Coast

To claim your **FREE** report and DVD (valued $97) go to
www.biddingbuzz.com/book

Life's Cruising...$9,300 Profit Per Month For Less Than 1 Hr a Day Work

Three weeks ago we decided at the last minute to go for a holiday in Thailand. It happened on a Thursday afternoon where we booked flights and accommodation to fly out on the Saturday. Less than two days to prepare. Knowing we have an automated eBay business that can operate in any country, with your laptop and internet access, we knew that we could do it. How many 'jobs' or businesses will allow you to do that? Not many.

With all the training, expertise and support provided from Genta, the Bidding Buzz team and our mentors and JV partners, Matt and Amanda, anything is definitely possible. We managed to have all our orders fulfilled while we were away, thanks to the warehouse and fulfillment system we set up before going away. It just proves that you can travel overseas and still run your eBay business with less than 1 hour work per day.

We are on target to do about $9,300 profit this month, or about $48,000 in gross sales. We might have to wait until June to break $50,000 sales and $10,000 profit. I have attached some photos, some are the views from our various offices/rooms and celebrating reaching our goals in Thailand. As you can see from the photos, it was very hard to take...

Now planning the next trip...
Regards and Many Thanks, Geoff and Jenny

Peter Makes $11,683 in Just 7 Days Using Every Strategy, System and Tip, He Learnt From Matt & Amanda's eBay Magic System.

I invested in the eBay Magic Program around October 07 and followed every step and strategy. I put the effort in, spent the time finding my hot untapped market and basically did anything and everything Matt and Amanda suggested. I was so serious about this that at one stage I was ringing the help desk daily for advice and got the help I needed every single time.

Last week alone, I did a massive $11,683 in sales in just 7 days. The only problem is...I can hardly keep up with the demand! You have no idea how excited I am and how addictive eBay is once you know what you're doing. This would never have happened without the eBay Magic system and the personal help I get all the time from Matt & Amanda and the Bidding Buzz team.

Thanks guys...we're wrapped with the results and we know we're heading for a very profitable year!

Pete and Theresa Bradley, Gold Coast

To claim your **FREE** report and DVD (valued $97) go to
www.biddingbuzz.com/book

$12,000 In Sales In Just 30 Days!

We would like to thank Matt and Amanda for their expertise they have shared with us during the Joint Venture Program. After two weeks of launching our product on eBay, we found that the product wasn't selling. So we arranged to have a conference call with Matt. After applying the strategies that Matt has taught us in just one phone call, we achieved Silver Power Seller Status within on month!!!

Our sales have reached over $12,000 a month and growing fast.

That's all within just 30 days! We are now the number 1 seller in our category.

We are so impressed by Matt's willingness to comb through little details, his strong analytical mind and his ability to fine tune the business and achieve outstanding result.
The knowledge & insight from Matt and Amanda are so powerful and we wouldn't do it any other way. Our whole experience with Matt and Amanda and the Bidding Buzz team is very pleasant and highly productive.

Thank you once again to Matt & Amanda and the Bidding Buzz team!!

Sincerely,

Pia & Warren

Peter Makes $6,000 Profit Per Month Working Less Than 1 Hr A Day On His eBay Business.

Hi my name is Peter Cutforth and I must say that we've been really wrapped with the results we've had from the eBay Magic course. After attending their 3 day seminar, seeing them live on stage and seeing everything they were doing, in November 2007 we got serious. We found our niche and our suppliers and it's now February 2008 and we're making a net profit of $6,000 a month. My wife spends one hour a day doing the postage and I spend less time than that just answering the odd questions. This is just the beginning and over the next three months we see our profits moving up to $10,000 a month at least.

It's been the perfect extra income stream for us and the course has been very easy to implement

Thanks

Matt and Amanda

To claim your **FREE** report and DVD (valued $97) go to
www.biddingbuzz.com/book

Rosanne Makes $4,000 In 3 Weeks After Attending the eBay Magic Workshop

Hi my name's Rosanne and three weeks ago I went to Matt and Amanda's 3 day workshop on the Gold Coast. While I was there, all the lights went on in my head. In the past 3 weeks since leaving the seminar I have made $4000 in my eBay business.

Rosanne Thrower, QLD, Australia

Darryl Young Now Makes $50,000 A Month With eBay Magic

Hi my name's Daryl Young and I'm a student of Matt and Amanda's. I got their eBay Magic course about 3 months ago. In my first week I made over $1000 profit and done over $100,000 in sales over the past 3 months. Last month I sold $50,000 of goods. I'm not even using a fraction of the system to it's potential yet and I can't wait to see what's ahead and launch some new products.

Thanks for all your help.

Married Homemaker Mother Of Three Makes $1500 In First Weeks

This is the best money I have spent on myself to date. Within 1 month of starting the eBay Magic course I'd made $1500 and that was just the kids room! Now I don't even have to think about school fees this term.

Wait till I get to that garage!

5 weeks into it, I've now found the product that I'm going to source and sell long term, thanks to Matt & Amanda's help.

By August I'll be making enough money so that my husband Matt can cut hours & the real living will begin for us as a family. Because that IS what it's all about isn't it?

Thanks for always walking by my side Matt & Amanda, I can't say thank you enough!

To claim your **FREE** report and DVD (valued $97) go to
www.biddingbuzz.com/book

We Got eBay Fever Bad!!

Matt, Amanda,

Just a quick email update to let you both know we are *totally totally* blown over by selling on eBay now. (and it's all thanks to you guys)

We no longer sit watching TV at end of the day.

We now rush home to view bids on our listings.

We are now on first name terms with our local post office staff.

We watch your videos every spare minute, taking lots of notes.

We no longer listen to music in car, just "magic" CD's
but most of all.....

We Just get a *BUZZ* of excitement every sale we make.

This is our first real week of selling and we have made about *£80 ($168 approx.)* net profit already !, just from bits around the house.... amazing (and focusing on good customer service is keeping the feedback at 100%)

We are really hyped up now.... and this is just the start.

Thank you, Thank you, Thank you both.

Regards,
John and Sam, UK

Couple Become eBay POWERSELLERS Shortly After Attending The Workshop

Hi Amanda & Matt,

I just wanted to send you a quick email to let you know that our sales have more than doubled since we attended your Workshop. We have implemented all that we learnt from you and Matt and it works..., - and as of last night, we are now POWERSELLERS - its so exciting....

So a Big Thank you From Us

Sheridan & Steve

P.S. I am off to the Post Office with lots to post......

To claim your **FREE** report and DVD (valued $97) go to
www.biddingbuzz.com/book

Chapter 19
The eBay Icons, Abbreviations
And What They Mean To You

What Do All Those Abbreviations, Terms and Icons You See On eBay Mean?

Have you ever wondered what a particular eBay term, acronym, or icon means?

Have you ever been confused with all the different terms often found on eBay, and when chatting back and forth with other eBay members?

Don't worry, you're not alone!

Here's a list of them for you and it's very handy to have at hand. Because if you're an eBay 'newbie', half the time you won't have a clue what these abbreviations mean!

Having said that, even if you're not a 'newbie', you might not yet have encountered some of these terms.

B&W: Black and white

BC: Back cover

BIN: Buy It Now

EUC: Excellent used condition

FAQ: Frequently asked questions with the answers

FB: Feedback

To claim your **FREE** report and DVD (valued $97) go to
www.biddingbuzz.com/book

FC: Fine condition

FVF: Final Value Fee

G: Good condition

GU: Gently used

HP: Home page

HTF: Hard to find

HTML: Hyper Text Markup Language

IE: Internet Explorer

INIT: Initials

ISP: Internet Service Provider

LTD: Limited edition

MNT: Mint. Means perfect condition

MIB: Mint in box

MIJ: Made in Japan

MIMB: Mint in mint package

MNB: Mint no box

MOC: Mint on card

MOMC: Mint on mint card

MONMC: Mint on near mint card

MWBT: Mint with both tags

MWMT: Mint with mint tags

NARU: Not a registered user (or suspended user on eBay)

NBW: Never been worn

NC: No cover

NIB: New in box

NM: Near mint

NR: No reserve price for auction listing

NRFB: Never removed from box

NWT: New with tags

OEM: Original equipment manufacturer

OOP: Out of print

PM: Priority Mail

RET: Retired

SCR: Scratch

S/O: Sold out

Sig: Signature

SYI: Sell Your item form

TM: Trademark

UPI: Unpaid item

URL: Uniform Resource Locator. The address that identifies a website

USPS: United States Postal Service

VF: Very fine condition

VHTF: Very hard to find

WS: Widescreen

XL: Extra large

Now, let's go over some of the common terms and eBay glossary and what they mean. You'll be speaking the eBay language in no time at all!

Account Guard: The security feature of the eBay Toolbar. This feature identifies when toolbar users are on an eBay or PayPal Web site, and warns them when they're on a potentially fraudulent Web site. This feature also warns eBay users when they're about to give out their password to a non-eBay site. Here's where you can report anything suspicious.

Bid Increment: The amount a bid is raised in order for it to be accepted in the auction style listing. This amount is determined by the current highest bid. For example, if the current bid was at $5.00, the next bid would be at least $5.50

Category Listings: The categories by which items are organized on eBay. One of the most important ingredients when you're listing items for sale on eBay. If they're not in the correct category, it's unlikely anyone will even see them, yet alone bid on them! Learn everything you can about this area!

Completed Listings: Another very important area of eBay you'll need to understand for your success.

This is a search for all items in a particular category that have ended over the past 15 days on eBay. Fantastic tool for sellers wanting to know how a particular product is selling if they too are thinking of selling it!

Discussion Boards: This is an area where members go to post messages to the eBay community and all sorts of things.
You can ask questions, learn hot tips, share experiences, and connect with other like- minded eBay users.

Dispute Console: This is where buyers and sellers get help with issues such as Unpaid items and Items Not Received problems.

eBay Community: This is the area where you'll find groups of buyers and sellers who share a common interest. You'll see all sorts of announcements such as calendar events, discussion boards and help if you need it.

To claim your **FREE** report and DVD (valued $97) go to
www.biddingbuzz.com/book

eBay Stores: These are pages on eBay where you can showcase all the things you have for sale. It's like having your very own shop front! It's also a great place to maximize your sales and it's very cheap to list items in this area. Make the most of this area!

Escrow: This is where a third party holds a buyers payment in trust until the buyer receives and approves the item from the seller. This procedure is usually taken advantage of when people are buying very high-ticket items. This service is recommended for purchases over $500 or higher.

Be careful with this one…there are many shonky 'Escrow' services in the market place and eBay recommends that buyers and sellers use www.escrow.com as their chosen company.

If you do decide to use a different escrow company, make sure they are bonded and licensed.

Final Value Fee: This is the fee that eBay charges the seller once the listing has finished. Final value fees are determined by the end price the seller gets for an item. There is no fee charged to the seller if there are no bids on an item, or the highest bid didn't meet the seller's reserve price.

Guides: This is where eBay members write and share their information and expertise on a particular topic or category. A great way for sellers to let potential bidders know that they are knowledgeable in the products or services they are selling.

Insertion Fee: This is the fee that eBay charges the seller for listing an item. This fee varies, depending on the type of listing, and it's non-refundable.

Multiple Item Auction (Dutch Auction): A listing where the seller offers multiple, identical items for sale. With this type of auction, there can be many winners. Winning bids are determined by their overall value, which is the bid price, times the number of items bid on.

PayPal Buyer Protection: This is a protection program that offers buyers up to $20,000 of free coverage if they pay through PayPal on qualified listings. Listings are qualified if the seller has a feedback score of 50 (98% positive) and also meet other transaction-relation requirements.

Items that qualify for PayPal Buyer Protection are denoted by the PayPal Buyer Protection shield on the 'View item page'.

PowerSeller: A seller on eBay who has maintained a 98% positive feedback rating and provided a high level of service to buyers. When buyers see the icon next to the seller's User ID, they know they're dealing with an experienced, honest eBay seller. This is an icon that is worth having beside your seller User ID.

Proxy Bidding: This is where eBay automatically bids on the buyer's behalf, in an 'auction style' listing.
The buyer simply enters the maximum amount they're willing to spend on the item, and eBay will continue to bid incrementally for the buyer until either the buyer wins the auction or the maximum has been reached.

This is especially good if you don't want to hang around and watch the auction or simply can't sit there and bid for yourself!

Second Chance Offer: This is where a seller can make an offer to a non-winning bidder when either the winning bidder has failed to pay for the item, or the seller as more than one of the same item.
The seller has the chance to offer a Second Chance Offer immediately after the auction has ended, or up to 60 days after the completion of the auction.

eBay doesn't charge an insertion fee, but if your Second chance Offer is taken advantage of by the buyer, then you'll be charged a final value fee.

This is a fantastic way to get your profits soaring if you sell the same items over and over again!

We use this feature all the time and approximately 50% of our Second Chance Offers are taken advantage of by excited buyers who thought they were going to miss out on the item!
It's definitely a win-win-win situation for both the buyer, the seller and eBay!

Sell Similar item: A great feature that lets sellers list new items based on the information they've previously entered for another item. By choosing this option, eBay automatically transfers information from the old listing into the new one for easy editing.

Another great way to save time on writing listing copy that can otherwise take hours!

Seller's Assistant: Now here's a fantastic tool that can help sellers save hours of hard work. Seller's Assistant Basic helps frequent sellers create professional listings in bulk, track them at eBay, and manage customer correspondence.

Especially good for high-volume sellers. It comes with a 30 day free trial! What have you got to lose?

Selling Manager Pro: An awesome eBay selling tool that has many features to help you run your business more smoothly with less hassle! Features include…listing items in bulk, sending feedback and emails in bulk, and also generate profit and loss reports.

Shill Bidding: This is where the deliberate placing of bids to artificially raise the price of an item occurs. This is not good practice and if you're caught your account will likely be shut down…and rightly so!

Shill bidding undermines trust within the eBay community and is most definitely NOT permitted. To avoid the appearance of involvement in this type of activity, family members, friends, roommates, people living together or sharing the same computer should not bid on each other's items.

Sniping: This is where buyers place bids moments or seconds away from the auction ending. Sometimes it appears that no-one is bidding on an item and then in the last few seconds of the auction, many bids appear all at once!

If you're a seller, there's nothing more exciting to see, but if you're a buyer trying to win the auction, this can be very frustrating. There are even sniping software programs on the market to do this for you!! A good way to avoid being outbid, if you're the buyer, is to simply place your highest bid and let eBay bid for you!

To claim your **FREE** report and DVD (valued $97) go to
www.biddingbuzz.com/book

Turbo Lister: A great advanced eBay selling tool that helps sellers create multiple listings quickly and easily on their computer. This is a desktop-based application.

You create your listings on your computer and then upload them to eBay when you're ready. Fantastic if you can't get online and you want to prepare your listings anywhere, anytime!

> *"Its in moments of decision your destiny is created."*

Darren J Stephens
International Bestselling Author & Speaker

All it takes is a click!

All it takes is a click!

Do you want to make your business more efficient? Then maybe you should just Click and Send!

With Australia Post's Click and Send you can prepare your documentation, pay online and organise courier pick up, all from the convenience of your desk! eBay sellers can import sold items automatically into Click and Send to prepare them for postage, all online.

As an eBay seller, you can register on Click and Send using a link from your "My eBay" page, and link your accounts.

Following this, whenever your eBay items are sold, the item data is automatically imported into Click and Send. From there, the Click and Send process operates as per usual – using the imported data to create address labels, offering payment options online or instore, and enabling online courier pick-up bookings if required.

This helps you minimise data entry and makes order processing much faster. The great thing about Click and Send is that you can prepare all the documentation you need to send parcels online – and if you're sending lots of the same item, or multiple items to the same address, you can access this information at the click of a button, instead of having to re-type it again and again.

Click and Send guides you through a step-by-step process and ensures that all the required information is correctly incorporated into the final delivery documentation that you print out.

To claim your **FREE** report and DVD (valued $97) go to
www.biddingbuzz.com/book

First you are prompted to enter all the necessary information, then select your preferred delivery service. You then choose either to book a courier pickup online, or simply print out the prepared documentation and take the items to your local post office.

Depending on your selections, payment can be made online by credit card or Australia Post account, or you can just pay at your post office if you prefer.

For more information, or to register
for Click And Send visit:
auspost.com.au / clickandsend

Quick ways to make sending easier!

The five steps to sending overseas with Click and Send:

1. Enter or import the delivery data required into Click and Send and choose which delivery service suits you best.

2. Book a courier online if required.

3. Choose how you'd like to pay (Account, Credit Card, or Pay at Post).

4. Print out the delivery documentation, sign it and attach it to the item.

5. Hand the item to the Messenger Post Courier if booked, or take it to your post office.

Other Great Benefits

If you choose sign up and become a registered user (which takes a minute or two), you can also access the following benefits:

Import addresses

Each time you type in a new address, you can save it to your address book. Or, even more conveniently, you can import a file from you existing database and it will instantly populate your address book.

To claim your **FREE** report and DVD (valued $97) go to
www.biddingbuzz.com/book

From there, you just need to click on the relevant address anytime you are sending an item and it will automatically populate the necessary fields.

Import shipment data

If you already have all of the shipment information in a spreadsheet or in another sales system, you can use the Import Wizard to import the entire spreadsheet into Click and Send, and it will automatically populate the necessary fields.

Generate detailed, customised reports

You can create reports accessing delivery data as far as three months back, which can be perfect for keeping internal audit records about what has been sent. These reports are customised and can be viewed onscreen, or exported so you can use them as required. You can also run the reports as required, or set to run on a regular basis and be emailed to you.

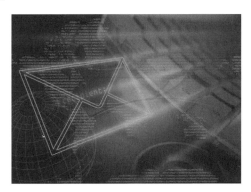

Email proof of shipment

All domestic items and Express International items can be provided with proof of shipment. Simply email the item details and a link to Australia Post's tracking site to the sender or a third party through Click and Send.

For more information, or to register
for Click And Send visit:
auspost.com.au/clickandsend

Track items

For all domestic items and for Express Courier International or Express Post International, you can track your items online once they have been lodged.

Send email pre-alerts to let customers know their item is on the way

Click and Send will send you an email with full details about your transactions each time you use it. If you would like to inform your customers that their item is on the way, you can use the "email notification" tab to set up this handy function. Emails can be prepared in five different languages.

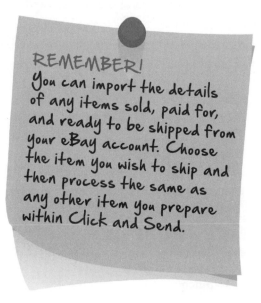

REMEMBER!
You can import the details of any items sold, paid for, and ready to be shipped from your eBay account. Choose the item you wish to ship and then process the same as any other item you prepare within Click and Send.

To claim your **FREE** report and DVD (valued $97) go to
www.biddingbuzz.com/book

nd your parcels online with
ck and Send today!

ustralia Post's Click and Send service you can prepare documentation, pay online and organise courier all from the convenience of your desk. As an eBay seller, you can register via Click and Send and link your count so that your sold item(s) information is automatically imported into Click and Send." By using d Send you minimise your data entry, and make order processing more efficient.

r now at auspost.com.au/clickandsend

f every day.

About the Authors

MATT CLARKSON

When Matt Clarkson left school at 16 to become a hands on carpenter the last place you would expect him to end up is running a multinational business specialising in eBay education, but that's exactly what happened.

After initially spending 15 years working in the construction industry on projects ranging from simple homes, mega mansions, high rise commercial buildings and block buster film sets; Matt is now a bestselling author and international expert in Internet Marketing and in particular eBay business development.

His previous experience in construction and Project Management of multimillion dollar mining and construction projects, has enabled him to manage and grow Bidding Buzz from a home based business into a multimillion dollar company in only 3 fast paced years.

After realizing that he needed to make changes in his life and wanting to forge into a brand new industry, Matt and his partner Amanda began selling on eBay in early 2006 and quickly established themselves as one of Australia's fastest growing eBay businesses.

They had actually created one of the world's leading eBay business systems, enabling people to establish and automate their eBay business up to 90%. It was only a matter of time before they knew they had to share this system with the world and quickly built Bidding Buzz into a global corporation, with successful and happy customers all over the world.

Now with students in Australia, the United States, the United Kingdom, Ireland, Hong Kong, Indonesia, Sweden, Malaysia and beyond, with a support team of 16 staff members, Matt along with Amanda, is leading the Bidding Buzz phenomenon across the globe. The future is looking bright not only for Bidding Buzz, but for the thousands of people who have now studied their eBay business systems and are making positive changes for themselves and their families.

To claim your **FREE** report and DVD (valued $97) go to
www.biddingbuzz.com/book

AMANDA CLARKSON

Amanda is a passionate entrepreneur who left school at age 16 and has had 33 jobs and has gone on to establish and run 11 businesses over the last 20 years.

Amanda's eBay business, which she started with a credit card in Feb 06 was a run away success and is still forging ahead to this day. Now, along with her husband Matt, she shows everyday people how to become cash and time rich with eBay through their simple, and inspiring eBay education courses.

This amazing journey has seen her now present to thousands of people, from all walks of life, ages and backgrounds around the world, including Australia, London and America.

As a result, everyday people are now living the 'eBay lifestyle' enjoying more time and more income for themselves and their families.

Her deep desire to help and inspire people to improve their lives both financially and personally, coupled with the powerful Bidding Buzz eBay education programs, has driven her to the top of the business and online community around the world.

Amanda's vision is to help as many people as possible live life more on their own terms instead of someone else's through The Magic Of Making Money On eBay.

FREE BONUS

To Claim Your
FREE Report, Your
DVD & Special
Audio MP3 Gift
With A Total Value
of **$297** visit...

www.biddingbuzz.com/book